MURDER & MAYHEM
— IN —
PRESCOTT

DREW DESMOND AND BRADLEY G. COURTNEY

THE
History
PRESS

Published by The History Press
Charleston, SC
www.historypress.com

Front cover, top left: courtesy Sharlot Hall Museum; *top center*: Sharlot Hall Museum; *top right*: Sharlot Hall Museum; bottom: Sharlot Hall Museum. *Back cover*: courtesy www.visitwhc.org; *inset*: courtesy www.visitwhc.org.

First published 2020

Manufactured in the United States

ISBN 9781467144322

Library of Congress Control Number: 2020938642

CONTENTS

ACKNOWLEDGEMENTS

Although many people have been encouragements to Drew Desmond, three particularly stand out. First is my coauthor, Bradley G. Courtney. I deeply appreciate your help, guidance and friendship and look forward to sharing Prescott's wonderful history. Second is Patricia Ireland-Williams. Your early support and belief in my writing are profound. You are the one who put me on the social media map, and I am most grateful. Last and most important is my wife, Pam. You not only encourage and nurture my writing, but without you, this joyful chapter of my life would not have even started.

Bradley wants to thank Drew Desmond, whose name is cooler than his. Thank you for this opportunity to coauthor with you. I cherish your friendship and know we will continue to get the word out about our hometown's fabulous history. Susan Tone, your enthusiastic editing is something I never want to be without. Sue Kissel, thank you again for stepping in with research that I was unable to do myself. Wendi, I love you and the life we have created together. Your support is incomparable and greatly appreciated. Joshua and Lindsay, you are the best son and daughter a father could ever hope for. I love you both so much.

1

VIOLENCE FINDS ITS WAY INTO EARLY WHISKEY ROW'S POPULAR DIANA SALOON

By Bradley G. Courtney

In July 1868, Albert Noyes, owner and operator of the Quartz Mountain Sawmill—Prescott's first sawmill—announced that a large building would soon grace Prescott, the likes of which the four-year-old hamlet had never seen. He soon began its construction on the southwest corner of Montezuma and Gurley Streets, where Hotel St. Michael stands today.

While the structure was being built, locals marveled at the size of the frame. Noyes reported that it would be a 60-by-28-foot, two-story building, nearly 3,400 square feet in total. The upstairs would be used for fraternal organizations such as the Masons and Odd Fellows. The downstairs would be a first-class saloon.

Sometime in October, and after overcoming several setbacks, Noyes's "mammoth" edifice was completed. Townspeople predicted that it would be "an ornament to the town" and anticipated "some Jolly old times inside its glittering walls."

The original plan was to rent the downstairs to Cal Jackson, a saloon man and a carpenter who was responsible for erecting some of Prescott's first buildings. That plan was scrapped. Andrew Moeller coughed up $8,500 and purchased Noyes's handiwork in early November 1864.

A transplant from Chambersburg, Pennsylvania, Andrew Lucian "Doc" Moeller, like many, headed west during the California Gold Rush of 1849. After Abraham Lincoln declared Arizona a U.S. territory in 1863, Moeller journeyed to Arizona and landed first in its northwest corner, which would later become Mohave County. After hearing that better things were happening in the Central Arizona Highlands, Moeller moved there. In late 1864, he was hired as a bartender in William Hardy's brand-new Quartz Rock Saloon on Granite Street. Moeller's prospects began to brighten.

As a property owner, he would soon become nearly unrivaled in Prescott. His first purchase was the Quartz Rock Saloon in 1867 after bartending there for nearly three years. During the 1870s, he owned at least twenty-seven lots throughout town and was bringing in $1,000 a month in rentals, worth more than $22,000 by today's standards.

The new meeting hall and saloon on the corner of Montezuma and Gurley Streets became Moeller's most famous property. It can honestly be said that by becoming the proprietor of the legendary Quartz Rock and then establishing a grand, first-rate saloon on the corner of Montezuma and Gurley— it would become known as the Diana Saloon—Andrew Moeller became the father of Prescott's famous, and sometimes infamous, Whiskey Row. A row of saloons would go up south of the Diana, which became the cornerstone of that row, named after the beverage that many in Prescott detested.

Around 4:00 a.m. on September 20, 1869, two men were shot dead and one seriously wounded in the Diana. The

Albert Noyes erected the "mammoth" building on the southwest corner of Montezuma and Gurley Streets that became the Diana Saloon. *Sharlot Hall Museum.*

Andrew Moeller opened the Diana Saloon in late 1868. A row of saloons soon followed. *Sharlot Hall Museum.*

September 25 edition of the *Arizona Miner* reported this tragic incident as "the bloodiest in the annals of this town." The killed and wounded men were active soldiers from Fort Whipple, a military post north of Prescott.

The *Arizona Miner*, Prescott's first newspaper, reported the town's early violent episodes from its headquarters on South Montezuma Street. *Sharlot Hall Museum.*

Sergeant Patrick McGovern of the Eighth Cavalry had been shot dead, as had Private Thomas Donahue of the Twelfth Infantry. Private George Nunes of the Twelfth Infantry suffered a knife wound.

Why the fight started was not divulged, but whiskey—as it often was—was behind it all.

Three men were accused: Private Harry Langham, also with the Twelfth Infantry, and two discharged soldiers, Joseph Johnson and William Collins. Langham, who had stabbed Nunes and was suspected of killing Donahue, was caught and arrested that morning. Eyewitnesses claimed that it was Johnson who shot McGovern. Collins was believed to have aided Johnson.

Both men fled the Diana and hurried south. A veteran of the Indian Wars, Lieutenant William McCleave, led the Eighth Cavalry in pursuit of the fugitives. The *Miner* made it clear that "it is the prayer of this entire community that they will be killed or captured."

The military posse followed a trail that led south through the Bradshaw Mountains and then into the McDowell Mountains. The Eighth Cavalry stopped to resupply at Fort McDowell. There, they wisely acquired several Pima Indian scouts. McCleave and his men followed the Pimas into the farms of the Salt River Valley. The trail became hotter in the Sacaton Mountains about fifty miles south.

In the hills above the Little Gila River and near the Sacaton Station, a former stopping point along the Butterfield Overland Mail Route, Johnson and Collins were trapped and captured on October 8. Unhesitatingly, McCleave credited the Pima scouts.

The Eighth Cavalry turned the accused men over to authorities at Fort McDowell. On October 14, Lieutenant D.A. Kane and his troops brought the prisoners to John Taylor, Yavapai County sheriff, who lodged them in the county jail.

A week later, a party of Pima Indians showed up in Prescott. Their intentions were to get what they deserved: payment for their part in capturing Johnson and Collins.

The grand jury trial of Joseph Johnson and William Collins was scheduled for the first week of May 1870. On Tuesday night, April 26, Sheriff Taylor made sure his prisoners were securely locked up before calling it a day. Apparently, the jailhouse had no night guard. Johnson and Collins were sharing a cell made primarily of wood. Somehow, their friends on the outside had sneaked a saw and auger to the jail mates, who were able to hide the tools.

Wednesday morning rolled around, and Sheriff Taylor returned to the jail to find a sizable hole in the rear wall of Johnson and Collins's cell. They had sawed and drilled a section out of the wall, crawled through it and then escaped with an ease that troubled Prescottonians. It was the first jailbreak in their little town's history. Taylor immediately announced a $300 reward for the six-foot, black-eyed Johnson and $200 for the shorter, blue-eyed, light-skinned Collins. They were never caught.

After the Diana slayings of September 20, 1869, violent crimes became more commonplace along the Row. Most were fueled by whiskey, and most took place in or at least began in a saloon. Some locals wished there were no saloons at all in their young town and that "every drop of whisky on the continent was in Africa or China."

In the very late autumn of 1869, Sheriff Taylor was strolling down Montezuma Street when a shot was heard. The bullet passed right through his coat sleeve. The shooter was not known at the time, but on Tuesday evening, December 7, that changed. Taylor was called to an unidentified Whiskey Row saloon. A soldier identified only as Pegan had drank too much "punching whiskey" there and was picking fights.

Taylor arrested him. On the way to jail, Pegan's tongue became as loose as his fists had been clenched. He bragged that it was he who had taken the potshot at the sheriff and came "within an ace of making himself a murderer." He was fined fifty dollars for drunken behavior and released, much to the disappointment of those who knew of Pegan's dangerous behavior.

This was merely a prelude to another night of horror at the Diana.

In the early summer of 1870, a notorious desperado, Hiram Lightner, was staying in Prescott. On Wednesday night, June 29, he decided to visit its most popular watering hole, the Diana. Lightner became engaged in a game of faro with Sion Bradley, a forty-something professional gambler from Missouri. Bradley also had a drinking problem. He also had a reputation for being an honorable man, and some even felt he was "the best pistol shot on the Pacific Coast."

At some point, something went wrong. Lightner and Bradley began quarreling. Lightner reached his boiling point and pulled a pistol and began shooting at Bradley. Four shots left his gun—plenty to show that murder was intended. Bradley, the intoxicated and noted pistoleer, was unarmed for a change and completely defenseless. One bullet went astray. Three struck Lightner's target. One egregious bullet hit Bradley in the groin and then passed through his bladder.

Drs. George Kendall and James McCandless were called to the scene. An impromptu operating room was set up in the Diana. Working together, the doctors successfully extracted the bullets, but Bradley's condition was critical.

Lightner had escaped. A physical description was published: "Lightner is about 5 feet 10 inches in height, of sandy complexion; wore Burnsides whiskers; had on a chequered shirt and pants made of material resembling corduroy. He is a very bad man." Bradley hung on for six days. He finally succumbed during the early morning of July 5.

Hiram Lightner turned himself in on Independence Day, just hours before Bradley passed away.

Bradley's death was used as a cautionary tale in the fight against the two most despised vices in Prescott: "His fate should be a warning to other men who are following the same course of life—gambling and drinking—for, sooner or later, it will lead them into trouble."

2

WILLIAM JENNINGS

PRESCOTT'S HERO AND INSANE MAN FROM THE HASSAYAMPA

By Bradley G. Courtney

Following the Diana slayings and several other violent episodes along Whiskey Row, the town leaders felt Prescott was deeply troubled and going in the wrong direction, perhaps even headed toward a ghost-town status. One suggested solution was establishing the position of night watchman. This would not be a position secured by an appointment or election. Rather, it would be paid for by a pool of Prescott businessmen.

Prescott has had its share of legendary lawmen. The first peace officer to really make a difference was William Jennings, a transplanted Englishman who was not a marshal, sheriff or chief of police. Hired in 1871, he was the town's original night watchman. By 1872, his reputation was rock solid. After one shooting incident on Granite Street, it was reported that "Jennings was on hand, *as usual,* [italics added] and put a stop to it."

Like Whiskey Row, Granite Street (one street west of Montezuma Street) was a common source of early trouble. Another major incident occurred on that dirt road in March 1873. Around 11:00 p.m. one evening, Jennings, a fearless one-man police force, heard a shot. Believing it had come from a Granite Street brothel, he raced toward the sound. On arrival, he saw some soldiers attempting to bust through the bordello windows. Jennings ordered them to stop, but they kept trying to break in.

À la Wyatt Earp, Jennings pistol-whipped one soldier into submission, making an example of him. That prompted the others to stop; they didn't want to get hurt like their friend. Jennings then lit a match, by

---

WILLIAM JENNINGS,

NIGHT WATCHMAN.

Attends to Calls at all Hours.

William Jennings advertised his "business card" in the *Miner. Bradley G. Courtney.*

means of which he discovered that a soldier had been shot and was clearly in critical condition. He obtained medical help, which was given in the gunman's house. Subsequently, the wounded soldier was taken by wagon to Fort Whipple.

The shooter was arrested. He was a former cook at Fort Whipple who had made several enemies there. The wounded soldier's friends were aiming to kill the shooter that evening. Had Jennings not showed up, this surely would have happened.

Law enforcement by pistol butt was used again in the fall of 1873. A man, again on Granite Street, had assaulted a woman with a hatchet. Jennings arrived and disarmed the man by shooting him through the hand that was holding the hatchet. He then used the butt of his pistol to placate the attacker with a swift and sure blow to his nose.

Prescottonians felt safer with Jennings roaming the streets at night. It was reported in the *Miner* that "Prescott brags on her nightwatchman, Mr. Wm. Jennings, who knows so well how to preserve the peace and watch over the lives and property of his sleeping brothers and sisters."

William Jennings was the hero of Prescott in the early and mid-1870s. But because of a sudden change in behavior, his heroics would be overshadowed starting in 1877. His downfall would be more precipitous than his ascension.

All heroes have an Achilles heel; Jennings was no exception to this rule. When armed with enough money, he could inveterately be found gambling at a faro table in a Whiskey Row saloon. In fact, soon after Jennings had taken the night watchman job in early 1871, the *Miner* reported that he had "quit in disgust, because he could not make a fortune by watching and bucking the tiger [a phrase for playing faro]." But either he was persuaded or he came to his senses. He stayed on the job.

But his gambling habit proved too much. During the early morning of November 23, 1877, he was in a Whiskey Row establishment playing faro.

What transpired in the saloon toward the end of those games is unknown, but at some point things went awry.

After leaving the saloon, Jennings was walking down Montezuma Street with Frank Murray, the village marshal. Suddenly, Larry Tullock, the faro dealer, was seen running out of the saloon toward Jennings. Tullock began to rebuke Jennings so vehemently over some perceived offense that Murray felt it necessary to arrest and cuff him.

Then the unthinkable happened. As Murray was walking the faro dealer to jail, Jennings quickly drew his knife and lunged at Tullock with the aim of stabbing him in the stomach. Murray swung and lifted Tullock away. Jennings's knife, however, landed deep in one of Tullock's thighs.

Tullock was carted off to obtain medical attention. Jennings was arrested and immediately fired as night watchman. For several years, it was difficult to keep that challenging position filled. Even Virgil Earp gave the job a shot, but he resigned after about a month's time.

Jennings was sentenced to six months in prison in January 1878. While imprisoned, he began showing signs of mental disturbance. He was seeing spirits and hearing voices.

Still, after his release, the irrepressible Jennings quickly made news in a positive manner. He discovered that his gift for finding gold was even greater than his noteworthy talent for law enforcement. Jennings had claimed prime mining property south of Prescott next to the Hassayampa River and built a cabin there. Time and again, the *Miner* published reports like the following: "Jennings is in from his Hassayampa bonanzas, which are numerous and rich."

Some believed that if his good luck continued, he could become the richest man in the territory.

Jennings had another vice: drinking whiskey. In early April 1879, after picking up supplies at the Bashford General Store, Jennings left for his cabin but "was detained at several points" along Whiskey Row. Nightfall arrived, and an inebriated Jennings finally pointed his two burros south. A mile or two from town, he fell from his mount and passed out in the middle of the road. The next morning, his burros were still with him, but he had been robbed of everything else. The *Miner* poked fun at him by stating that perhaps the robbers had "administered chloroform or some other stupefying drug."

By early July 1879, Jennings's Midas ways were in the news again. It was reported that he was a true "bonanza king" and described as having "mineral in front of him and mineral in the rear of him."

However, along with his prosperity, Jennings continued to show signs of further mental illness. They surfaced most visibly in September 1882. The

Courier reported that he was "now a little 'off' in his mind." His reputation grew as "the insane man from the Hassayampa."

His paranoia caused him to believe he had nearby enemies who were trying to poison him. When one neighbor visited Jennings's well next to the Hassayampa River in September 1882, Jennings shot at him. The formerly celebrated night watchman was soon arrested and taken to the insane asylum in Stockton, California.

Jennings did not return to his home by the Hassayampa until sometime in 1884. His success as a gold miner continued for another eight years.

As time went by, however, the living legend became more reclusive. Because of this, after he had not been seen in Prescott for two weeks during the second half of September 1892, there were no immediate worries. His neighbors, however, eventually became concerned and decided to check in on him. One later rode into town and reported that a body had been spotted at the bottom of a 110-foot mine on Jennings's property.

A close friend of Jennings's, Dan Hatz, traveled out to recover the body. It was found sitting upright on the mine's deepest bench. It was clear that Jennings had been there for some time.

Thus ended the life of one of Prescott's first heroes, the man who became "the well known and eccentric miner of the Hassayampa."

3

MURDER—OR WAS IT?—
ON MONTEZUMA STREET

By Bradley G. Courtney

Another Man Shot" read the *Arizona Weekly Miner* headline of September 21, 1872.

The late 1860s and early 1870s were treacherous times in Prescott. As mentioned in the previous chapter, there was so much mayhem in Prescott during those years that many were concerned about the town's survival.

This shooting was different. First, it was not whiskey-fueled, like the majority of the other shootings that occurred along Whiskey Row. And, on the surface, the men involved—especially the shooter—were of a seemingly higher caliber, unlike the drinkers and gamblers usually found hoisting fists or guns or other weapons. William Hellings, a respected Phoenix businessman and one of the valley's most influential founding citizens, shot Edwin Grover, his former business partner and close friend. The Hellings and Grover families were even connected by marriage in some way.

William Brelsford Hellings was born and raised in Philadelphia. After serving as a clerk for several civilian sutlers who sold provisions to Union army soldiers in the field during the Civil War—and eventually working as a sutler himself during the war—Hellings made his way west in that same capacity, aiding soldiers dealing with the so-called Indian problem.

Hellings's entrepreneurial and adventurous spirit brought him to Fort Yuma on the Colorado River in 1869. There, the thirty-something Pennsylvanian operated as a post trader. In the spring of 1870, he arrived at Camp McDowell, twenty-three miles northeast of today's Phoenix,

Arizona, and opened another trading post that was "the finest, best stocked establishment of its kind in the Territory."

In a nearby settlement, Hellings also opened a wholesale-retail store and won contracts to supply grain and other farm crops to military camps and forts throughout the territory. As if he was not busy enough, he also obtained a federal license that enabled him to trade with several Arizona Indian tribes. All of this was under the auspices of W.B. Hellings & Company.

When Hellings arrived in what is now the Phoenix area, the Salt River Valley was developing as the major agricultural center for Arizona Territory. He was recognized as a man of prominence and served on the committee responsible for choosing the townsite that would become Phoenix.

Hellings's business ideas became more ambitious. While Phoenix was forming its roots, he partnered with his brother Edward, as well as Cyrus Grubb and Edwin Grover—his future victim—to establish the Salt River Flouring Mill along the banks of the Swilling Canal (named after Jack Swilling, often cited as a founder of Phoenix) in late 1871.

The Salt River Flouring Mill was enormously successful and quickly became the largest mill in the territory. It supplied flour and grain to military posts, Indian reservations and other communities throughout Arizona. The mill generated staggering profits at times. There were reports that in some months the mill made more than $30,000 in profits (in the tens of millions by today's standards).

Edwin Grover was born in Maryland but moved with his parents to Philadelphia at a young age. There, he became friends with Hellings. The *Miner* reported that they had "been intimate friends for many years past, sleeping under the same roof and eating at the same table." How the two childhood friends connected in Arizona is unknown.

A key character and source of dispute in the shooting incident in Prescott was William's brother Edward, eight years younger and twin-like in appearance. Edward joined William at Camp McDowell in September 1870, serving as clerk and bookkeeper for his brother's expanding enterprises. Eventually, he was appointed superintendent of the Salt River Flouring Mill in 1871.

The Hellings brothers' partnership with Grover and Grubb was short-lived, probably ending in mid-1872. Why? It is not definitively known, but it is possible the breakup centered on Edward's role as supervisor of the Salt River Flouring Mill. The brothers continued to operate the mill and their other businesses on their own until they added a third partner, Major Charles H. Veil. He was a former army officer who had served honorably during the

Apache Wars, which were still ongoing. Veil probably met William Hellings during his post trading days.

On the night of September 19, 1872, Hellings encountered his former business partners Edwin Grover and Cyrus Grubb along a portion of Montezuma Street that was becoming known as Whiskey Row. Prior to this, Grover had allegedly insulted William's brother by calling Edward a "son of a bitch." William was greatly angered over this slander.

Although it was undetermined how they would do this, William Hellings claimed that he and Grover had agreed to "settle the matter" the next time they met, which turned out to be September 19 on Montezuma Street. Whether or not this was a chance encounter was never established in court. The evidence points to the likelihood that it was.

Between ten and eleven o'clock that night, Grover and Grubb left the Nifty Saloon and began walking south along Montezuma. In front of the News Depot, an argument broke out between Grover and Hellings. Hellings testified that he assumed Grover would be armed because of their prior decision to resolve this one way or another when they next met. William demanded—twice, according to Grubb—that Grover take back the insults aimed at his brother. Grover steadfastly refused to recant.

Hellings then thought Grover made a move to pull a gun because he had moved his hands toward his back. Hellings yanked out his pistol. Grover twisted to his left, and Hellings pulled the trigger. The bullet entered below Grover's right shoulder blade, penetrated his right lung and exited to cause a wound above his left wrist. He collapsed on the sidewalk.

Bleeding profusely, Grover was taken to the nearby Jackson & Tompkins' Saloon and attended by Dr. J.N. McCandless on a makeshift bed. Later, he was transferred to his rented room, where McCandless and a Fort Whipple doctor, Bernard Semig, treated him.

Hellings immediately turned himself in to a Yavapai County deputy sheriff, who detained him. Hellings was charged with "assault with a deadly weapon with the intent to commit murder." That became subject to judicial change on October 1 after Grover died of his wounds. Hellings had already been released from the county jail after posting $10,000 bail, but now he would have to forfeit his freedom and return while a jury decided if he should be charged for murder.

John A. Rush, one of the top criminal lawyers in the territory, represented Hellings. A native Missourian, Rush was among the throng of men who had traveled west during the California Gold Rush. He even practiced law in the newly christened Golden State. He came to Prescott near its inception, and,

Before William Hellings pulled the trigger, Edwin Grover twisted to his left. *Courtesy of Gary Melvin.*

by 1867, was the acting attorney general for Arizona Territory and attorney for the Third Judicial District.

The district court's prosecutor, James E. McCaffry of Tucson, was another heavyweight lawyer. A product of Baltimore, Maryland, McCaffry also had been afflicted with gold fever and drawn to California in the mid-1800s. When called on to prosecute Hellings, he was serving as U.S. attorney for Arizona Territory and as Pima County attorney.

In June 1873, McCaffry presented the facts related to Grover's killing to a jury of Yavapai County men. Seeking to prove Hellings a murderer, he called ten witnesses. Nevertheless, the jury was not convinced. Hellings, to the surprise of some, was not indicted for Grover's murder. For now, the case against him was dropped. Hellings returned his attention to his business enterprises.

Killing a man—alas, even a former close childhood friend—did not slow him down.

The flourishing Salt River Flouring Mill was now being managed by Major Veil. With the distraction of nearly being tried for murder out of the way, Hellings used the time to construct what became perhaps his greatest accomplishment. He planned to create a consortium of business leaders with the goal of building a wagon road through Black Canyon from Phoenix to Prescott but discovered that he and his associates would have to go it alone.

Hellings and his team blazed a road through Black Canyon in less than three months' time, an incredible feat. It was opened for travel in November 1873. A milestone for Arizona, Black Canyon Wagon Road cut in half the time and distance from Phoenix to Prescott and became the favored route over the more western route that existed at the time through Skull Valley and Wickenburg. Hellings's reputation as a mover and shaker in the territory grew.

The good times would be postponed. Justice Charles Tweed and the Third Judicial District were not finished investigating Grover's death. In the same month the Black Canyon Wagon Road was completed, Tweed approved a grand jury request to reconsider the non-indictment decision regarding Hellings five months earlier. On November 13, that ruling was overturned and Hellings was again arrested "for the crime of murder." He was quickly released after a $10,000 bail was posted by brother Edward and friends, one of whom was Morris Goldwater, uncle of Barry Goldwater.

Hellings's response to the indictment was swift and assertive. He entered a not guilty plea and asked for a change of venue for the upcoming trial because he believed his personal enemies in Yavapai County were "manufacturing public sentiment and creating prejudice of bias against him, with a view of procuring his conviction." Some prominent Yavapai County citizens supported this motion. The court agreed with Hellings and moved the case to Maricopa County, his home turf.

Hellings also moved to obtain the testimony of the doctors who had attended to Grover after the shooting. This was granted. Dr. Semig delivered this deposition on January 9, 1874:

> Q. *In speaking of him being shot under the shoulder, did you ask him if he did not twist himself around as the shot was fired; if so what was his reply?*
>
> A. *I did ask him the question, and he replied, "that was the way I was shot."*
>
> Q. *Did you make use of the following language to him, to wit; Now Grover, tell me the truth, why did you raise your hands; did you intend to shoot, or what did you intend to do, or words to that effect?*
>
> A. *I did so address him and he replied—well that ain't for me to say. I cannot tell nor do I know what I would have done. I made a mistake in Bill Hellings.*

Q. From the general tone of the conversation with Grover, and his manner at the time, would you infer that he intended to fight?

A. I would.

Q. Do you know anything in regard to Grover's pistol being found fast or entangled in his pocket?

A. I do not, only from hearsay.

Q. Did Grover make any direct reply to you in answer to the question, as to why he raised his hands?

A. He did not; he tried to avoid the question.

Semig's testimony could have been used two ways. The prosecution could say that, by twisting away from the pointed gun, it proved that Grover was trying to get away. However, because Grover had twisted "as the shot was fired," it gave the defense ammunition that Hellings did not purposelessly and cowardly shoot Grover in the back, which had been documented and suggested at the coroner's inquest. Also, it more than hints that Grover did indeed intend to fight Hellings. Hellings may have perceived this intention, and the impulse to pull the trigger was thus provoked.

The trial, *Territory of Arizona v. William B. Hellings*, was calendared for April 23, 1874, in Maricopa County. Several Prescottonians were subpoenaed. Some were not happy that they would have to leave their businesses and travel this long distance. One witness, editor John Marion of the *Miner*, wrote cantankerously, "We, being one of the victims, will suffer considerable pecuniary loss by having to hire someone to edit the MINER in our absence."

A few Prescott witnesses did not show when April 23 came around. Justice Tweed ordered the arrest of the defaulters. The Yavapai County sheriff was then told to bring them down by April 27, the date the case was set to continue. After the shirkers were given a proper scolding and ordered to remain available or suffer further consequences, the trial began. Only one witness, by the prosecution, was called that day.

The only other witness to the killing besides Hellings was Cyrus Grubb, and he was missing. He was not in Prescott but in Fort Vancouver, Washington Territory. He had moved there several months before the trial. Had he bolted to avoid testifying against Hellings, his former associate?

The first key issue of the trial was whether Grover had made a threatening move toward Hellings, prompting him to defend himself. That brought up the question of whether Grover was armed. Perhaps even more critical, had there really been an understanding about settling the matter of the insult the next time the two met, even if by happenchance? If true, what did that mean? Was there an assumption by both that they would be carrying guns and that there would be a fight or a duel of some sort?

It was asserted that Grover left behind a dying statement, defined as "a statement made by a person who, at the time the statement was made, is conscious of the fact that his death is near or certain. The law recognizes a dying declaration as an exception to the hearsay rule and allows for its admissibility at trial."

This document apparently did indeed exist. However, the court refused to admit it into evidence, most likely because of a technical legal issue. It may have been missing a statement that Grover knew he would soon die. It may have been tainted or tampered with in some way. At one point, the defense attorney himself, John Rush, curiously offered to have Grover's dying statement read to the court and jury, claiming that his client did not want to be cleared of murder because of a technicality. Perhaps even more mystifying, the prosecution objected, and the court sustained it.

The defense called six witnesses, the most important of which was Hellings himself. There is no court record available to show exactly what he gave as testimony, but we can assume that self-defense was the focal point. The defense focused not on whether Grover was armed, but that it was assumed by Hellings that Grover did have a gun in his coat.

Then there was the question, Did Hellings shoot Grover in the back? That question was probably answered via the deposition given by Dr. Semig on January 9, 1874, cited earlier. His claim was that Grover admitted that he "had twist[ed] himself around *as the shot was fired* [italics added]." This gave credence to the assertion that Hellings did not purposely shoot Grover in the back—even though the ball first entered through his right shoulder blade—thereby indicating it was not outright murder. Also, as discussed earlier, Grover told Semig that he did indeed intend to fight that night, although it never became clear as to how he intended to do so.

The defense rested its case on April 30. When the prosecution rested, it had not presented a particularly strong case. After closing arguments, the jury retired to deliberate. It took only five minutes to return with a verdict of not guilty; there was not much evidence other than what supported the conclusion of self-defense. Spectators applauded, and Hellings was the recipient of many handshakes. It took some time before order could be restored in the court.

Whether Cyrus Grubb's testimony would have altered the verdict is a matter of speculation. He had given a deposition on October 2, 1872, one day after

Grover's death. However, he was silent on the issue of whether Grover had made a move that could have been interpreted by Hellings that he was drawing a gun.

It is possible that neither the prosecution nor the defense wanted Grubb's testimony, not knowing how he would testify regarding the key matter of self-defense. Furthermore, because he was living in Fort Vancouver, Washington Territory, outside of the jurisdiction of the court, there was no legal process at the time to force Grubb to appear at Hellings's trial.

It is questionable that merely calling Edward Hellings a "son of a bitch" was the only reason that provoked his older brother into pulling a gun and shooting Grover. It was a common enough insult and not one that usually resulted in men shooting one another. Was there something more to the breakup of the business partners and friendship? Were there some dishonest actions rendered by the two brothers, or vice versa?

A contributing factor may have been William Hellings's temperament. It was said that he could be a very charming man, but it was also purported that he had a tendency toward anger and arrogance. Was there a darker side to him?

In June 1870, there was a minor federal tax matter involving Hellings. He believed that he had been scammed and accused a U.S. attorney of being a liar and an unmitigated scoundrel and that the U.S. attorney should be tarred and feathered, tied to a cactus and escorted out of town to the desert "to the music of The Rogue's March." There is indeed a revealing murderous anger in that statement.

As for the rest of the story, Hellings continued to prosper. Whatever was said about the man, it is clear that he practiced a bold and entrepreneurial modus operandi that benefitted Arizona. In spite of temporary setbacks, every one of his projects eventually led to success—even after the accusation of murder.

Hellings lost a legal dispute in 1876 with Charles Veil after losing ownership of the flour mills in Phoenix. He turned to the mining industry, in which he invested heavily. At one time or another, he owned or operated silver, gold and copper mines in Maricopa, Yavapai and Pinal Counties. These enabled him to form a corporation via a group of investors. This was groundbreaking for the day. It would eventually become the way things worked in the West. Hellings ushered in an era of speculative eastern investment in western mining claims.

Domestically, he was not as successful. He changed marital partners three times, but every marriage ended in failure.

William Hellings died in Mint Valley, California, on July 3, 1913. He had escaped the gallows but left a productive mark on the early commercial development in Arizona Territory.

4

VIRGIL EARP JOINS POSSE
THAT KILLS TWO OUTLAWS

By Bradley G. Courtney

So great is the shadow cast by Tombstone's famous 1881 shootout at the OK Corral that it is not widely known that the law-enforcement career of Virgil Earp began in Prescott, Arizona.

In 1877, the Jackson & Tompkins' Saloon on South Montezuma Street, near the center of Whiskey Row, was one of the top four saloons in Prescott. On October 17 of that year, Colonel William McCall—a Pennsylvanian who had been breveted general during the Civil War—was enjoying a game of billiards therein. That is when two men, George Wilson (calling himself "Mr. Vaughn") and Robert Tullos (aka John Tallos), walked in and made a beeline for McCall. One jabbed a pistol in his back; the other whispered threats in the colonel's ear.

Why? Eight years prior, McCall had been living near the Texas/Oklahoma border. While there, he learned that George Wilson had murdered Robert Broaddus, a deputy sheriff in Montague County, Texas. Most likely, McCall played a part in the attempted apprehension of Wilson, who proved elusive. The murderer fled to Colorado before eventually journeying to Prescott. To his surprise, Wilson spotted McCall in the saloon. Knowing McCall was aware of his crime, Wilson was afraid the colonel might cause him trouble.

Somehow, McCall escaped Jackson & Tompkins' and rushed straight into the office of Justice of the Peace C.F. Cate and reported the presence of the outlaws. Cate issued an arrest warrant for "Mr. Vaughn" and "John Doe"; Tullos was a stranger to McCall. The warrant was given

Whiskey Row as it appeared when Virgil Earp lived in Prescott. *Sharlot Hall Museum.*

to Constable Frank Murray, who immediately strode over to Jackson & Tompkins', followed by McCall.

Prior to their arrival, the two no-goods—clearly soused—stepped outside. One took a potshot at a dog being walked by a lady along Prescott's center-of-town plaza. When Murray arrived, that was the offense for which Wilson and Tullos believed they were being arrested. After being told otherwise, both drew their pistols, quickly mounted up and galloped their horses down Montezuma Street while shooting to the left and right, like a scene from a Western movie.

Murray then gathered an all-star posse. But it took some time—perhaps up to an hour—giving the desperadoes a head start.

Somewhere in Prescott, three men were engaged in friendly conversation, apparently far enough away that they were oblivious to what was transpiring downtown. Two were high-ranking lawmen. One was Yavapai County sheriff Ed Bowers, who, along with Murray, would pursue on horseback. The other was U.S. Marshal Wiley Standefer. He and McCall hopped aboard a horse-drawn carriage.

The third was Virgil Earp, new to Prescott and so little known that its newspaper, the *Weekly Arizona Miner*, called him "Mr. Earb." Most historians agree that Virgil had never been an official lawman up to this point, but he was toting his Winchester rifle. Given the situation, it might come in handy.

Virgil was promptly deputized. However, he presently had no horse, and there was room for only two on the carriage. He would have to keep up on foot!

Wilson and Tullos were expected to be far down the trail by now. How long would Virgil last? Fortunately for Virgil, the chase would not be a long, arduous, Western movie–like affair, but more like an act from Mel Brooks's *Blazing Saddles*.

The outlaws, instead of distancing themselves from Prescott, stopped about a half mile (perhaps less) southwest of the Row, probably on the corner of Carleton and Granite Streets by Prescott's main waterway, Granite Creek. Both dismounted with pistols pulled and waited while smoking cigarettes.

Standefer and McCall, leading the posse and moving fast, rode right by the fugitives. Lucky break for the outlaws? Yes, until one of them shouted, "Don't run over us, you son of a bitch!" The two posse members halted and turned their guns on the bad men while Murray and Bowers rode down and did the same. Earp quickly caught up, positioned himself between the other lawmen and shouldered his Winchester.

After hearing the demand to surrender, Wilson vociferously entreated God to have mercy on his "poor drunken, worthless" soul.

The criminals opened fire.

Bullets and buckshot came from three directions. Wilson fell immediately when a bullet penetrated his skull. Tullos died instantly after being shot eight times, almost all from Virgil's Winchester.

To the astonishment of many, George Wilson hung on for two days with a bullet in his skull before finally succumbing. The *Miner* boys became theological during those two days, wondering if the prayer Wilson had bellowed before being shot would have any effect because of the sincerity behind it, even with its profanity: "It was the language with which he was familiar. The question is, are not such earnest prayers as likely to be answered as those hypocritically expressed in more elegant phrase?"

An interesting side note and piece of trivia to this story is that Virgil's younger brother, Wyatt, had dealt with Wilson in Wichita, Kansas, in 1875, when he was a policeman there. Apparently, Wilson had "forgotten" to pay for a wagon he had acquired. Wyatt came to collect.

It was later learned that Wilson was an even more debauched man than first thought. He was also wanted for the murders of the sheriff and deputy of Las Animas County, Colorado.

This episode proved to the people of Prescott that Virgil was a man who could be counted on. He was soon appointed Prescott's night watchman and was later elected constable.

Late in 1879—after a series of letters between the brothers—Wyatt and older brother James arrived in Prescott with their wives. John Henry "Doc" Holliday and Mária Katalin Horony, aka Big Nose Kate, arrived soon after. In late 1879, Virgil, Wyatt and Morgan Earp, as well as Holliday (after eight months of living and gambling in Prescott), gathered in Arizona Territory's newest boomtown, Tombstone. On October 26, 1881, in a thirty-second gunfight, they shot their way to a level of long-lasting fame they could have never imagined.

MURDER IN THE NEW PALACE SALOON

BY BRADLEY G. COURTNEY

Six weeks after the new Palace Saloon opened in July 1884—the original on Goodwin Street had burned down that February—it was baptized with murder. Fred Glover, a former bouncer at the Diana Saloon who later became "a dissolute gambler and an irreclaimable opium fiend," brutally killed his lover there on Thursday, August 28. The *Courier* labeled it "Dickensian."

Glover had been working at the Sazerac Saloon on Gurley Street but had also become financially dependent on his lover, Jennie Clark. Clark was a prostitute whose real name was Nellie Coyle. She was described as "a comely woman of not more than 26 years old, of frail and delicate frame." Although regarded as a "social outcast," it was thought by some that she had been raised in a more genteel environment; her behavior had a bit of sophistication to it.

Jennie was also sick with consumption and already closer to death than most folks. Clark and the thirty-something Glover lived together in an apartment at madam Mamie Pearson's bordello on Granite Street.

Rather than going straight home after getting off earlier than expected on August 28, Glover headed around the corner to Prescott's current hot spot, the Palace Saloon at 118 South Montezuma Street. Reports suggested that Glover did not go home right away, because he was angry. He had begged Jennie that morning to give him $100. She refused.

At half past midnight, Jennie decided to look for him. She grabbed her best friend, Dora Palmer. They crossed Whiskey Row Alley, walked straight into the Palace and cajoled him into coming home. As the two prepared for bed, Jennie saw how sloshed Glover was and, much to Glover's chagrin, decided it was her turn to have some of that kind of fun. She and Dora went back to the Palace and began drinking—heavily, according to witnesses.

Glover, in the meantime, got out of bed and set out to do more barhopping on his own. By the time he returned to the Palace, he was even more intoxicated than before. And he had two acquaintances with him, Jim Carruthers and a Mr. Harris.

When they walked in, there on the music stage was Jennie, singing her heart out while Dora accompanied her on the piano. Glover and Harris began heckling Jennie. Her hurt feelings caused her to cry out, "Damn it, you needn't make fun of me!"

Glover and his buddies moved to the end of the Palace's walnut bar and invited Jennie and Dora to join them. Jennie's response was, "No, I won't drink with a damned son of a bitch." Persons nearby were not sure if this comment was directed at Glover or Harris. Soon, however, Jennie and Harris were exchanging insults and crudities, Jennie giving as good as she was taking. Instead of supporting his girlfriend, Glover defended Harris, accusing her of being too harsh on him.

Soon Jennie and Glover were nose-to-nose and shouting at each other. Someone pushed first, maybe Jennie, but it was Jennie who wound up on the Palace floor. Bartenders Piercy and Vogt stepped in, and Jennie took refuge behind the bar. While there, she grabbed a bottle of soda water and threw it at Glover and Harris. Glover fired back by hurling several bar glasses at her.

The bartenders were somehow able to gain temporary control. When Jennie returned to the bar and put her hand to her head, she discovered she had a gash. She screamed, "My God, my head!" More insults flew back and forth between Jennie and the two men, so Glover knocked her to the floor again. Jennie cried for help, but this time, no one came to her rescue.

There was a man named John Ellis present who was running for sheriff. He was later shamed in the newspapers for not stepping in while a woman was getting beaten.

Jennie was able to get back to her feet. She then turned her venom on Harris, who responded by knocking her to the floor for a third time. This time, Glover helped her up. He walked her over to the south wall to continue their argument in imagined privacy. But both were too drunk, too angry and too loud.

Jennie bellowed that she would never love Glover again, especially after she had supported him not only financially but also after many of his friends had deserted him. Continuing to scream, she became more enraged with every remembrance. Jennie then shrieked, "Damn you, strike me if you dare!" She then hit Glover in the face. Glover retaliated, connecting with a punch that knocked her to the floor for the fourth and final time.

After shouting at her—"Damn you, let's see how you faint now, and do it pretty!"—he began kicking frail Jennie, stomping her over and over on the head, neck and chest. Jim Carruthers finally intervened, crying out, "Damn it, my mother was a woman and I can't stand seeing a woman stamped!" He and another man pulled Jennie away from Glover.

But now, she appeared to be unconscious.

Jennie was carried home, apparently with Glover's help. Fifteen minutes later, around three o'clock that Friday morning, Jennie Clark died.

Glover was suddenly overcome with remorse, weeping over his lover's beaten and dead body. He then hurried over to the house of James Dodson, the chief of police, and woke him to desperately tell Dodson that he, Glover, was being accused of killing Jennie but was innocent. Dodson calmed him down and told him to go home. He would look into the situation as soon as possible.

Glover returned to the Palace. After seeing Jennie dead in her apartment, Dodson tracked down Glover and took him into custody. Word spread around Prescott that a woman had been beaten to death. A call went out for Glover's lynching. Wiser minds prevailed. The *Courier* chided the angry souls, assuring them that, surely, a fair trial would be held and "the hangman's services will be again necessary to purify the moral atmosphere and vindicate the outraged majority."

The next day, Jennie Clark was buried in an unmarked grave in the Citizens Cemetery. Glover had sought permission to attend the burial but was denied. He wept in jail the entire day. A few women—all of Clark's profession—followed her casket to the cemetery.

It did not take long for Glover to be tried and sentenced to hang for first-degree murder. A successful appeal to Governor Frederick Tritle changed his sentence to life in prison. The next year, Governor Meyer Zulick granted Glover clemency. Life imprisonment then became a ten-year sentence. Things continued to get better for the convict. In 1890, Governor Nathan Oakes Murphy inexplicably pardoned him. Glover was set free on December 20, 1890. He had served only six years.

In mid-January 1891, Fred Glover was seen once more in Prescott. He was en route to Seattle and was never heard from again.

THE CURSE OF THE KEYSTONE SALOON

By Bradley G. Courtney

T he Keystone Saloon was situated in that area of early Whiskey Row that bled north onto Cortez Street (there were times during Prescott's history when Whiskey Row was more than the quarter-city block it is today). If any Whiskey Row saloon was cursed, it was the Keystone. Its ill-fated reputation began in 1884, when a lightning bolt struck and destroyed the barn attached to it. Everything in the barn was destroyed, including two horses that were stabled there.

The real curse, however, began with its first proprietor. Gotlieb Urfer came to America from the canton of Bern, Switzerland, sometime before the American Civil War. He arrived in Prescott in 1874, opened a lodging house on Cortez in 1877 and married Ellen Dunn of Ireland in 1878. In 1882, Urfer bought the Arizona Brewery on Gurley Street facing the plaza, one of Prescott's most popular gathering places. He eventually added a saloon to his lodging house and named it the Keystone Saloon and Lodging House. It became his primary business.

On Wednesday, December 16, 1885—one day before his fiftieth birthday—Urfer was found lying senseless on the floor of his saloon behind the bar, bleeding copiously from a bullet wound to the head.

A Keystone lodger had sprinted into the saloon at about six o'clock that evening after hearing the report of a pistol. He was not the first person on the scene. A distraught and unidentified African American man was standing at the bar. The lodger also noticed a revolver lying on the floor.

Looking behind the bar, he saw Urfer on the floor "with a great ghastly hole in the right side of his head, from which his brains and blood were oozing." When the lodger turned to ask the man what happened, he had already absconded. Several others who had been nearby also ran into the saloon after hearing the gunshot.

Therein they saw what the lodger was seeing, and "near [Urfer's] right hand, lay a pistol of the bull-dog pattern," a British-made pocket revolver—the same make used to assassinate President James Garfield in 1881. Those first on the scene, save for the Keystone lodger, immediately concluded that this was a suicide.

Urfer's death made people scratch their heads and wonder. What reasons did he have to stick a gun to his head and pull the trigger? There were no signs he was on a path leading to such a horrendous terminus. Especially stupefying was that Urfer had been busily, even excitedly, preparing for a grand celebration to be held in the Keystone. A few days before his death, an announcement appeared in the *Miner* exposing not only his plans but also his apparent positive state of mind: "Gotlieb Urfer, the genial host of a lodging house and saloon, will celebrate his fiftieth birthday on Thursday, December 17th, and feels so jolly over the event that he wants all his friends to call and partake of a lunch which he will spread, from 1 o'clock to 4."

Friends said that he had even been talking about how he would seat his guests.

On December 16, just before the fatal shot was heard from the Keystone, he was preparing for the next day's feast. With Urfer was George Hook, whom Urfer asked to run out to buy some eggs. Ellen Urfer had stepped out a short time before. Less than five minutes later, Gotlieb Urfer was lying on the floor of his saloon in a pool of his own blood.

The physical evidence provided no other conclusion—Urfer's death was self-inflicted. The African American who had been seen standing over Urfer surely bolted because of the way it looked.

A short time after Urfer's suicide, an unidentified lodger made the same choice, but with a different method: suicide by swallowing poison.

The Keystone curse had only just begun. The drama would intensify. John McCarron, Urfer's best friend, handled his estate. He then took over the Keystone's proprietorship. That's not all he took. Less than a year later, on Monday, November 14, 1886, McCarron married Urfer's widow, Ellen. The *Miner* made sure to mention that McCarron's friends—and Urfer's—were stunned that he had married "Mrs. Urfer." Incidentally, the bride and groom were both considered very wealthy.

Eight months later, another gruesome episode occurred in the Keystone Saloon with way too much déjà vu. Around 2:00 p.m. on Saturday, July 9, 1887, the crack of a gun was once again heard coming from the Keystone. Seconds later, another shot rang out. Passersby on Cortez ran in to see what the ruckus was all about. There lay Ellen McCarron's second husband "with a ghastly hole in his right temple, from which his brains and life's blood lay fast oozing," less than ten feet from where his predecessor had shot himself through the head eighteen months earlier.

McCarron's choice of weapon was an antiquated cap-and-ball revolver with a barrel nearly a foot long. Oscar Vanderbilt was the first on the scene. On seeing McCarron's condition, he rushed to get medical help and found it in a Dr. Robinson. When the doctor arrived, McCarron was still breathing, but heavily. Death rattled in his throat. Forty-five minutes after he had shot a bullet into his brain, McCarron expired.

The note McCarron left behind was shocking. More than that, it was telling. It undoubtedly explained why Urfer had killed himself a year and a half before. It read, "I, John McCarron, am going to commit suicide; kill my wife and then kill myself. All caused by woman's abuse."

It appeared that McCarron intended to fulfill both declarations. A friend named McIntyre had been visiting McCarron frequently and divulged that the saloon owner had been drinking heavily as of late. During one conversation, McCarron, in his drunkenness, spoke of his wife affectionately but followed it by pulling his pistol from his pocket and stating that "it will be my doom."

On Saturday, July 9, McIntyre overheard McCarron asking the former Mrs. Urfer if she would like to accompany him on a buggy ride. She declined, excusing herself by claiming she was too busy. That decision probably saved her life. Apparently, it was now or never for McCarron. Shortly after McIntyre left, McCarron walked into his saloon with his revolver. The first shot from his pistol missed his mark widely, as if he was checking to see if his gun was working properly. The bullet passed high up on one of the saloon's walls and then through the ceiling before landing outside. The second shot penetrated McCarron's skull.

Almost hilariously, the oddities continued when McCarron's body was buried next to Urfer's in Prescott's Citizens Cemetery. The *Miner*, with blatant sarcasm, stated that the twice-widowed Ellen Dunn now had "two little mounds to keep green and to strew flowers over." The now-infamous lady married once more and became Mrs. Cronin. Her third husband, a laborer named James, somehow outlived the incomparable nag by twenty years.

Ellen Dunn's husbands, Gotlieb Urfer and John McCarron, committed suicide and are buried side-by-side in Prescott's Citizens Cemetery. *Courtesy of Norman Fisk.*

The Keystone Saloon survived. One would think it had accommodated enough death. However, although three suicides had taken place there, it had yet to host a homicide. That would change eight years later because of a dispute over seventy-five cents. Once again, some called it the most atrocious act ever perpetrated in Prescott up to that time. It was indeed abominable.

Charles Hobart had previously lived and worked in Prescott as a porter at the Scopel Hotel on the corner of Montezuma and Goodwin Streets. He had been arrested for robbery in February 1895 but was given some leniency—no jail time. Hobart was only required to leave town. This he did, but he returned to Prescott on Wednesday, October 23, of that year. Apparently, the law did not notice.

Hobart found a vacant room in the lodging quarters of the Keystone and paid in advance a total of one dollar, reserving four nights at twenty-five cents each, to John Miller, its new proprietor. During the night, Hobart's behavior turned repulsive: he "soiled the room." Of course, this irked Miller—described as "one of the most quiet, peaceable and inoffensive men living"—especially after Hobart reneged the next morning on his four-night reservation and demanded reimbursement for his unused nights, which amounted to seventy-five cents.

Miller refused. That amount would be the fee, he said, for having "to clean the room in the condition it was in when [Hobart] left it." Hobart then pulled out his sawed-off Winchester rifle, pointed it at Miller and demanded a refund. Somehow, Miller was able to slip away. He went straight to Chief of Police Steve Prince and reported the incident.

Prince found Hobart and immediately took him into custody. That same afternoon, Hobart stood trial. He was convicted only of drunk and disorderly conduct and fined five dollars. Clearly, he was not so short of money as to be in need of an extra seventy-five cents. He paid his fine and was released.

Peculiarly, even though his gun was initially confiscated, it was returned to Hobart. Apparently, the fact that Hobart was not supposed to be in town was ignored, or not known.

Hobart immediately took to the streets. Toting his Winchester, he attracted ample attention. Hobart first visited the Kelly & Stephens store on the corner of Gurley and Montezuma. There, he bought some woolen clothes because he had a long, cold ride ahead of him. So he told the people at the store.

Hobart's next stop was the Palace Saloon. There, he started drinking. At some point, he glanced at a clock and announced it was time for the "shooting match" to take place. When asked what that meant, he bluntly stated that he was going to kill John Miller before eight o'clock. Those at the Palace did not take the threat seriously and did nothing.

Hobart was not done drinking. He rode his horse up Montezuma, turned right on Gurley and headed to the Sazerac Saloon, where he continued the same threats. The Sazerac's Chinese chef, John Ross, overheard them and, knowing of the trouble between him and Miller, believed they were not products of hot air. Ross sent a messenger to Prince about this development.

Hobart, however, beat the chief of police to the Keystone. In fact, it may have taken an unfortunate amount of time to get the message to Prince. One witness later testified that he had seen Hobart looking for his dog outside of the Keystone.

Whiskey-crazed and angry, Hobart walked into the Keystone with his Winchester. Miller was facing the door, standing in the middle of the room between the bar and stove.

Keystone Saloon proprietor John Miller is buried in Citizens Cemetery within view of the graves of Gotlieb Urfer and John McCarron. *Courtesy of Norman Fisk.*

Hobart shouted, "Now Miller, you son of a bitch, I want your money or I'll kill you." He gave Miller no chance to respond. With his gun propped against his shoulder, Hobart fired. The bullet struck Miller directly in the lower throat. The saloon owner collapsed to the floor and, with blood gushing from his wound, took a few desperate gasps and expired.

Two men sitting at the Keystone bar witnessed the murder: Armstrong Roseberry and William Sachs. The startled Sachs stood up when the rifle was fired. Hobart did not like Sachs's movement, so he pointed the gun at him and warned, "If you move you son of a bitch, I'll kill you too." A click was heard as Hobart readied his rifle.

The gunman backed his way out onto the sidewalk, turned and, despite his pronounced intoxication, mounted his horse and galloped north on Cortez. He swung left onto Willis Street before heading up Granite Street and out of town. Eventually, Hobart turned and headed south.

Within ten minutes of Miller's death, Sheriff George Ruffner and his deputies began pursuit. Ruffner is arguably not only Arizona's most storied sheriff but also perhaps its most successful. This was not his most well-known pursuit of an outlaw but likely his first. The lanky, six-foot, four-inch Ruffner and his posse combed the countryside with no success. They rested at midnight.

Telegraph messages were sent to other Yavapai County lawmen to be on the lookout for a six-foot, one-inch, 180-pound man riding a small bay horse. Hobart had a "sandy complexion and sand moustache."

At daylight, the posse hit the trail again. Along the way, Ruffner and his posse picked up some Indian trackers. This proved to be a smart move. It was soon determined that Hobart was now on foot and heading south toward Phoenix.

By Saturday, a disoriented Hobart, thinking he was still on the road to Phoenix, had turned back toward the Bradshaw Mountains. On Sunday, his trail led to the Cy Curtis Ranch, on which stood a deserted house. Hobart was holed up there. When Ruffner and his posse learned this, the sheriff asked a man he had encountered along the way—a worker at the nearby Gladiator Mine—if he would make an attempt to goad Hobart from the house and into the open.

The miner acceded. His job would prove easier than anticipated. With the posse in hiding, the man approached the house but stopped at the well in front of it to take in some water. That is all it took to get Hobart outside.

With the Winchester he had used to kill Miller in hand, Hobart questioned the miner about where the nearby roads led. The conversation ended, and the miner sauntered away. Ruffner emerged from his hiding place and ordered Hobart to throw up his hands and surrender. Instead, the murderer raised his rifle.

Seeing this, Undersheriff Joseph Dillon shouted from the other direction. Hobart wheeled, but Dillon and other members of the posse beat him to the trigger. Shots came from several directions. Only one took effect: Dillon's buckshot knocked the rifle from Hobart's grasp and injured his right arm. John Miller's murderer surrendered.

By 11:00 p.m. that Sunday, Ruffner's posse and Hobart were back in Prescott. The accused "was given a hearty meal, which he ate with a relish." He was then locked up to stand trial, set for Wednesday, November 13.

Two lawyers were appointed to defend Hobart, but he refused their services. Hobart tried to appear insane before and during the trial, but no one bought his act. The testimonies of eyewitnesses Sachs and Roseberry were all it took to bring a guilty verdict. Hobart wept when given the sentence of life imprisonment.

7

THE DYNAMITE DEMON OF WHISKEY ROW

By Bradley G. Courtney

I t was called "a dastardly deed" and the work of a demon. In twenty-six years of Prescott history, it was the newest atrocity without parallel. By today's standards, it would be suspected as a terrorist-like attack. Even though the perpetrator had targeted only one person, he was willing to kill others in the process.

It was Sunday night, June 28, 1896. Without any indication that something might be amiss, an explosion detonated that was so powerful it shook nearly all the other buildings along Whiskey Row. It was heard throughout all of Prescott. The blast demolished a twenty-five-square-foot area in the Cabinet Saloon's dining room and damaged neighboring businesses: the Palace Barbershop and Al Dake's merchandise store. The Cabinet at this time was sited at 122 South Montezuma Street.

Minutes before the explosion, men were enjoying the usual delights offered inside the Cabinet Saloon: gambling, a spirited drink and conversation. The Cabinet was the heartbeat of early Whiskey Row and, during this time, was one of the two most popular saloons in Prescott. It would become the Palace Hotel and Bar after the fire of 1900.

In the rear of the Cabinet was a restaurant run by Chinese men, which was not unusual along Whiskey Row. Two ladies—"habitués of Granite street," which Prescottonians knew to mean they were prostitutes—were at a table in the dining area behind the saloon. One was Bertha Hovey, or at least that was the name she went by. Her companion was known only as Cora. Both were being served by a Chinese waiter.

The Cabinet Saloon can be seen at right-center in this image of Whiskey Row as it appeared in the 1890s. *Sharlot Hall Museum.*

At about twenty minutes before 10:00 p.m., just beneath Bertha and Cora's feet, there erupted a deafening explosion. Proprietor Barney Smith jumped to his feet. A frequent patron named Tom had been participating in a game of dice. He was known for having rheumatism but now seemed suddenly healed as he sprinted out the front door.

The head chef of the Chinese kitchen immediately thought the Cabinet was being attacked by Highbinders. He howled to the heavens for help. The Highbinders was a semi-secret Chinese society, mafia-like in that they were involved in criminal activities such as prostitution and blackmail. Some were hired assassins. Most of the Chinese in Prescott, understandably, feared the Highbinders who at times had indeed infiltrated Prescott's Chinatown on a small scale. The Highbinders would not have been happy that some of their own ethnicity were working for Anglo businessmen. But they did not cause an explosion on this night.

The explosion was so thunderous that hundreds outside the saloon rushed toward it to see what had happened.

All inside the Cabinet were dumbfounded. Some, including co-proprietor Barney Smith, suspected it was part of a robbery attempt, that the explosion was merely a planned distraction. Had robbers detonated the blast? Were they now waiting to pounce and scoop up any money or silver on the gambling tables or blown to the floor, or in the cash register? Smith ordered Frank Williams, the Cabinet's popular barkeep, to stay near the money just in case.

But that was not the situation. No robbers ran into the Cabinet that night.

After everyone gathered their wits, the damage was observed, which extended into the saloon. Anything that could move in the Cabinet had been displaced. Tables and chairs were knocked flat, glass from the windows and liquor bottles covered the floor and pieces of linoleum lay strewn everywhere. Those linoleum fragments would later tell a story.

The dining room and kitchen were destroyed, as was the back porch. The power of the blast was so strong that the one-thousand-pound oven in the Cabinet kitchen had been knocked over. Damages were later estimated at $1,000, which included $300 worth of imported liquors and a new $40 chandelier that had crashed to the ground.

It was obvious what had caused the explosion, and those present involved in mining work agreed that they were enveloped in a familiar odor. Dynamite fumes filled the air. In fact, some people mysteriously maintained that there had been an unusual odor in the air *before* the blast.

There was also no doubt that the death of someone, or more than one, had been the intention of whoever detonated this explosion.

Remarkably, the two soiled doves and the Chinese waiter survived. One of the ladies was harmed more than the other, but it was not clear which

The Cabinet Saloon's dining area, where Bill Binkley's dynamite exploded, was located where the southwest portion of today's famous Palace Restaurant and Saloon is today. *Courtesy of Norman Fisk.*

The Cabinet Saloon's bar, seen here, was badly damaged. The door to its dining area, where Bertha Hovey was sitting, can be seen in the back. *Sharlot Hall Museum.*

lady. "One of the women is laid up for repairs, while the other is as yet uninjured, but the Chinese waiter has a bad wound on one of his legs."

Considering the magnitude of the explosion and the collateral damages wreaked, their survival was deemed a miracle. Instant death would have been the expected result. In fact, neither lady had been thrown from the area in which they were sitting, and they did not realize at first that dynamite had been placed directly below them, or that they, or one of them, may have been the target.

There appeared to have been some science behind it. Someone thought about the bits of linoleum laying all over the wreckage. It was theorized later that the heavy layer of linoleum covering the restaurant floor had arrested the force of the blast and spread it to other areas. It was as if Bertha and Cora had been standing in the eye of the hurricane

Of course, the big questions were "Who?" and "Why?" Why would anyone want to blow up a perfectly fine saloon and restaurant? Chief of Police Steve Prince began an investigation.

After robbery of the Cabinet's gaming tables and cash register was eliminated as a motive, some facts came to light that could not be denied. One was that whoever perpetrated this act was familiar with the use and the power of dynamite, involved in the mining business perhaps.

Evidence began to suggest that maybe one or both of the ladies had been targeted. Bertha Hovey's "professional" colleagues mentioned to Prince that someone had indeed been stalking Bertha. They also revealed that she had not only a husband, but a jealous one. His name was William "Bill" Binkley. When questioned, Bertha, for reasons that later surfaced, claimed that, no, Bill could not be the dynamiter; the couple was "on pleasant terms."

Still, suspicion ran high. Prince arrested Binkley.

At first, Binkley asserted innocence, but he was unable to sustain his lie. On July 19, he confessed. He had quite a story to tell.

Binkley's motive was more than contempt for Bertha's profession, if he had any at all. Soon after they married, almost as if it had been a hoax, Bertha informed him that she had another husband. Whether Binkley and Bertha ever lived together is uncertain, but she had clearly arranged for them to live apart. Binkley confessed that he had stalked her "at her adobe" many times. Bertha, however, would belittle him and shoo him away.

Binkley felt emasculated, and his anger grew to a boiling point; he began planning a murder/suicide. He had been working at the Last Chance Mine in the Walker District. He was familiar with the use of "giant powder," and it was available for "free" at the Last Chance. Binkley procured six sticks of dynamite with three feet of fuse and one cap from a storage cabin there. He hid it behind the Double-Decker on Granite Street, which may have been Bertha's workplace, located just a few yards west of the Cabinet dining room.

Bill Binkley worked at the Last Chance Mine, seen here, where he stole dynamite to use in the murder attempt of his wife. *Sharlot Hall Museum.*

On the night of June 28, he learned where Bertha was sitting in the Cabinet. Taking his explosives to the Cabinet cellar, he placed them below his wife's table, lit the fuse and fled to the Royal Saloon down the street. Thirty seconds after he entered the Royal, the massive blast was heard across town.

Binkley followed the crowd to the scene of his crime. He later divulged that if he had seen Bertha dead, he would have followed "his mistress to the unknown." He was carrying laudanum, enough to fulfill that purpose. Seeing his once-beloved alive and that he had not supplied her with the ultimate lesson he desired to teach her, Binkley cancelled his planned self-inflicted death and walked off into the night.

After confessing to the crime, he tried to persuade the police chief to arrest Bertha for bigamy. Prince refused.

Binkley was convicted of attempted murder and sentenced to ten years in the Yuma Territorial Prison but was released after only three. He wasted no time and married Emily Garrison. They stayed together until she died eleven years later.

Again, Binkley wasted no time. Two months after Emily's passing, he married Rosina "Rose" Ward. The couple raised eight children together.

The Cabinet Saloon was back in business after a month of repairs following Bill Binkley's attempt to kill his wife via dynamite. *Sharlot Hall Museum.*

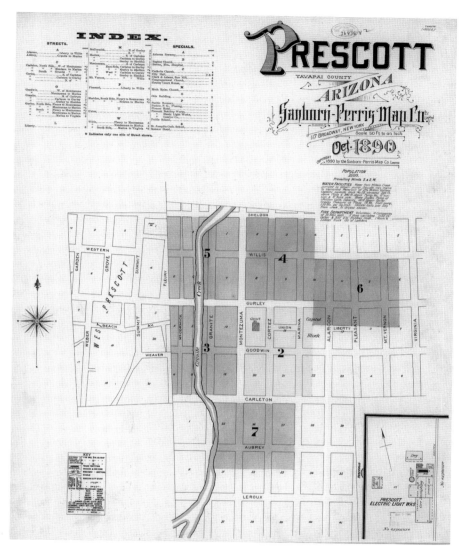

1890 Sanborn-Perris map of Prescott. *Courtesy WikiMedia Commons.*

According to Rose's granddaughter Terri Humble, one of their sons, Red, opened a saloon in Port Angeles, Washington, where at one point John Wayne was filming a movie. "John liked his booze so the two became very good friends," said Terri.

Bertha? Her fate is not known, but some believe she carried on with business as usual.

8

A MAKESHIFT UNDERGROUND TOURIST ATTRACTION

By Drew Desmond

It was a warm June 1904 evening. Jud Mullino was riding home with two companions, Frank Rahl and Frank Armour. It was at 5:30 p.m. on the twenty-fourth as they approached the Hicklin house.

As the three drew near, Fred Hicklin, Jud's drinking companion and fellow miner, came out of the house with a Winchester rifle. Inside was Fred's sister, Florence, whom Jud had been courting. Soon, the tranquility of the late afternoon would be ripped apart by the sound of a single rifle shot that would end up ruining three lives.

Instead of saying hello, Fred started stalking the three riders with his rifle pointed downward. Thinking that Fred's gestures were in jest, the horsemen mockingly put their hands up and started smiling and chuckling.

At once, Fred's rifle was raised and fired. The horses reared in shock. Frank Rahl would later testify that he "thought that [Fred] had fired at a bird or something, until he saw [Jud] fall from his horse to the ground." Fred's bullet had found Jud's heart. Jud fell on his back, with his arms outstretched, never to move again.

Rahl and Armour started toward the body when Florence appeared with a double-barrel shotgun. She shouted "that her brother killed that man, and she would shoot anyone who attempted to touch the body." The two turned to look at Fred, who appeared quite ready to fire another shot. They quickly left the area and rode to a nearby telephone office, where word of the shooting was sent to Prescott.

News quickly spread to the nearby McCabe Mine, and sentiment against Fred Hicklin mushroomed. Even in the Wild West, shooting an unarmed man who had his hands up was considered despicable and subhuman.

Fred's father, J.H., was headed back to the house when he heard the news and quickly rushed to the site. When he first came upon Jud's lifeless body, he said, "Young man, you got just what you deserved." He then turned to the crowd and explained: "This young man tried to seduce my daughter. If my son had not killed him, I would."

J.H. then procured a gun and sat at the front of the house, ready to fire on anyone who might "try to take Fred to lynch him."

When the deputy sheriff finally arrived at 9:30 p.m., he found a brooding crowd surrounding the Hicklin house. After hearing the account, the deputy sheriff arrested Fred and Florence in order to calm the horde. Still, public outrage did not abate until J.H. was later arrested for being an accessory to the murder.

Aside from the remark made by J.H. over Jud's body, none of the Hicklins gave any clue as to the reason for the sudden and severe change of feeling toward Jud before the trial. Speculation was rampant about what the Hicklins would offer in justification of the crime.

"One thing that is quite evident," the Prescott paper reported, "is that [Jud] had no warning of his impending fate and had no idea that [Fred] had any designs on his life."

A special grand jury quickly brought indictments, but the father's charges were later dropped. There was simply no evidence that he had conspired in the killing. His son Fred, however, was brought to trial just two and a half weeks after Jud's death.

The principal witnesses for the prosecution were Jud's two horseback companions. First on the stand was Frank Armour, who testified that when the shot was fired, "Jud Mullino reeled in his saddle, and plunged from his horse into the road."

"I was riding a colt," Armour continued, "which took fright at the sound of the gun, and whirled around. I looked back over my shoulder and saw [Jud] lying stretched on the ground on his back, with his arms extended. He was apparently dead."

Armour continued: "As my horse was plunging towards the Hicklin house I saw Florence Hicklin in the road ahead of me. She had a double-barreled shotgun in her hands. She told me not to go to the body or she would kill me. I looked back and saw Fred Hicklin with the rifle in his hands positioned for shooting. I then rode to the boarding house, and to the telephone office. I sent word of the shooting to Prescott."

Cross-examination failed to shake Armour's testimony. In fact, "evidence was brought out of a more damaging nature, as it was in direct contradiction to the story told later by the defendant himself," the paper noted. The witness said that Jud "was unarmed and he was in his shirt sleeves when shot."

Frank Rahl then took the stand and substantially confirmed Armour's account.

When Fred was called to testify in his own defense, the packed courtroom became electric with anticipation. Perhaps now the mystery about why the killing occurred would finally be revealed.

Fred testified that during the noon meal on the day of the shooting, Florence told him that Jud made "improper proposals" to her. When she declined his advances, Jud began to force himself upon her until "two parties came in sight." She told Jud that she would tell her brother, and he replied "that he could pack as big a gun as any of the Hicklin family." Fred stated that "her story had greatly enraged him and she was in an excited condition all afternoon." When Florence told Fred that Jud was approaching, Fred took his rifle and walked down the road. He testified that he asked Jud why he had insulted his sister and received no reply. Then Jud "made a sudden motion as if to draw a gun," Fred said, so he shot him.

When Florence Hicklin was placed on the stand, she confirmed Fred's story with further detail:

"I went out of the Marksbury house where I was on the Wednesday evening previous to the shooting, in company with Jud Mullino," she said. "We started out to find one of the Marksbury girls who had left the house. When about 200 or 300 yards from the house, Jud asked me to marry him. I told him I could not do that. I then said I would go back to the house. He then made an improper proposal to me and grabbed ahold of me. He threw me down on the ground and in the struggle, got my clothes up to my waist. I screamed several times. Then as he did not desist, I told him that my [other] brother Jim and Miss Marksbury were approaching. At that, he jumped to his feet and so did I. I then told him that he would see the day that he would be sorry for what he had done. I told him that I would tell my brothers about it. He told me to tell them that he carried as big a gun as they could pack."

On cross-examination, Florence admitted that she and Jud expected to meet one of the Marksbury girls near where she claimed to have been assaulted. She also admitted that she and Jud were headed to where she thought the girl would be found, "which negated very largely her entire story unless it is assumed that [Jud] was mentally unbalanced," the newspaper observed. If Jud was intending to assault her, why didn't he take her to a secluded place away from expected people?

Others who were there at the time of the alleged assault testified that they heard no screams from Florence and noted no disturbance at all. One of the most damaging witnesses against Florence's story was Eva Marksbury, with whom Florence spent the night on which the alleged assault occurred.

Eva stated that she was looking out of the window when Jud and Florence "came up together about 10 o'clock" that evening. She stated that she did not notice anything unusual in the actions of either or in "any disarrangements of Florence's clothing." Florence remained with Eva all night and "the two slept in the same bed."

Before they fell asleep, Florence related the conversation she had with Jud "but said nothing of the alleged attempt at outrage," Eva said. She also stated that she was within 150 steps of where the assault was supposed to have occurred, but that she did not hear any screams or noise of any kind. "The night was still," she said, "and there was no noise around them anywhere that would drown sound." The defense was unable to shake Eva's devastating testimony.

At this point in the proceedings, the defense realized the apparent hopelessness of its argument and asked to be allowed to introduce evidence showing that Fred was insane when he fired the shot. The motion was granted, and the defendant was again placed on the stand to testify as to his mental state. "In his testimony he probably convinced himself that he was really insane when he fired the fatal shot," the paper perceived, as he testified that "on the evening of the shooting I was very nervous. When the shot was fired something seemed to be pulling on the back of my head. My nerves were very much affected," he said.

However, Fred's cross-examination went terribly. He could not explain how, in his earlier testimony, he was able to recall such vivid and specific details during the time he now claimed to be insane.

Fred's parents were also called to testify to their son's mental derangement. Additionally, a doctor and a nun from Mercy Hospital testified to Fred having been treated for head injuries sustained when he fell down a shaft at the Iron King Mine.

After the defense had finished its insanity argument, the prosecution introduced a number of witnesses in rebuttal. Both Rahl and Armour testified that they saw no symptoms of insanity at the time of the shooting.

W.J. Shaw, who had appeared on the scene shortly after Jud was shot, testified that Fred, "instead of being agitated or excited, acted in such a cool manner that he thought it was some other man who shot Jud." W.J. stated that Fred "acted perfectly self-possessed and cool."

The verdict of the jury was guilty of murder in the second degree, with the recommendation to the court for mercy. He was sentenced to serve twenty to twenty-five years.

Eight months later, Fred was granted a new trial and attempted to use the argument of self-defense. However, since the first case demonstrated that Jud was unarmed and had his hands up, the appeal was quickly dismissed.

It was only a week after Fred's first trial that Florence had hers. "The trials of these cases attracted a great amount of interest in the community," the *Prescott Journal-Miner* reported, "probably on account of one of the defendants being a woman, and this being the first instance for years where a woman has been on trial in this county for her life." Indeed, the trials were extensively covered in out-of-town papers throughout Arizona as well.

The testimony in Florence's case was essentially the same as at the trial of her brother. Most newspapers reported the subject matter by employing euphemisms so thickly that they painted over the actual facts. It was the *Mohave County Miner*, primarily targeting an audience of the rugged digging men, that spoke simply and plainly: "In the trial of the girl it was set up that the murdered man attempted to rape the girl the evening prior to the murder, but no case was made out."

Florence was convicted of manslaughter. The Phoenix paper reported that "her story was disproved and the real cause of the killing was not divulged at the trial."

However, before sentence was passed, Florence's defense made a motion for a new trial, which was granted and would eventually win Florence her freedom. When the new trial came up, one of the main witnesses against her had absconded the area, and another had passed away a month prior. Therefore, the case was dismissed.

Her freedom secured, Florence made another attempt at love, marrying a man named John Putnam seven months later. "Either because the joys of wedded bliss were not to her liking or for other reasons not divulged," the *Arizona Republic* reported, "Mrs. John C Putnam, the bride of the day, left her husband at Arizona City yesterday morning, returning to him his wedding ring and announcing her intention to part with her spouse forever."

She had "quit her spouse after spending [only] one night under the roof he provided for her," the *Journal-Miner* stated, "taking refuge in the red light district of [Prescott]," where the profession was legal.

Due to her statewide notoriety, the nineteen-year-old became ridiculously popular—much like a makeshift underground tourist attraction. "She was later the cause of many disputes, which almost culminated in bloodshed," the Prescott paper recalled.

Two men, both piss-poor shots, got into an impotent gun scrape "over her affections." Since the paper made no mention of any long-term aspirations, it is presumed that the quarrel was over who was next in line!

Previously, two different men had entered Florence's room and stole what cash they could find. To them, the thirty-seven dollars taken was equal to an average man's monthly wages. To Florence, it was merely laying-around money. For Prescott's city fathers, the situation had become a little too notorious, and sometime during the spring of 1907, the law was sent to throw her out of town.

Howdy Pardner! How 'bout a date - - -

JULY 2-3-4

(For The Best Show On Earth)

Hassayampa Hotel
"PRESCOTT'S BEST"

This 1949 advertisement from the *Weekly Journal-Miner* shows that prostitution, although illegal, still thrived in Prescott, especially during Frontier Days. *Prescott Public Library.*

She took the train to the small station of Blanchard, the one closest to her childhood home, and continued plying her wares there. As her life spiraled downward, Florence also became intimate with liquor on a regular basis. Then, one evening in July 1907, she entered Blanchard's Grand View Saloon "crazed with drink, [and] engaged in an altercation with one of the visitors of the resort, threatening to take his life on account of some fancied grievance," the *Journal-Miner* stated. Her protest met total indifference, and in a rage, she went outside, took out a Colt .45 revolver and fired two shots through the building.

When she reentered the saloon, she must have been made aware that the sheriff's office was on its way to arrest her again. A drunken, hopeless despair began to set in. Already thinking that her life had hit rock bottom, Florence now stared directly into the abyss.

By this time, the mystery of the real motive for Jud's killing had leaked out, much to Florence's shame. She had only wished that Jud asked her to marry him. Instead, just the opposite occurred. He didn't ask for her hand in marriage, nor did he assault her. Instead, he informed her that he was leaving her in favor of another woman.

Florence was convinced that the only man she would ever love was dead, killed by her brother at her own urging. Perhaps she felt a desire to be with Jud.

"She seated herself by a card table in one of the corners of the place," the paper reported, "and resting her right arm carefully, placed the muzzle of [her Colt .45] revolver against the right side of her head just above her ear." Before anyone could make a move, patrons were horrified when she pulled the trigger and blew off the top of her skull. She was less than a mile from where Jud was killed and one month shy of her twenty-first birthday.

In the final analysis, the life of Jud Mullino and the cream of Fred Hicklin's life were snuffed out by the mere scorn of a teenage woman.

9

GRANNY GET YOUR GUN

BY DREW DESMOND

Sure, Joe Mackin had a few drinks, but that's not what was troubling him now. He stumbled into his house bleeding profusely from where seventeen buckshots had just shattered his shoulder blade. He told his wife that someone—a woman, he thought—had fired two shotgun rounds from the upper story of the Moses house.

His wife did her best to stanch the flow of blood, but it would be nine hours before Dr. J.B. McNally arrived to stabilize Joe enough for him to be taken to Mercy Hospital in Prescott to see if he would survive.

The year was 1912, and there had been trouble between Joe and his neighbor Fred Moses. Several weeks prior to the shooting, things had escalated to the point where Joe had begun to threaten Fred's life. Still, Fred's wife, Sarah, had midwifed Joe's newborn son, and now Joe reported that the baby was sick. He asked if Sarah could come with him to see what she could do. Fred was skeptical. He thought he smelled alcohol on Joe's breath, but if the newborn needed help, then Sarah, a fifty-two-year-old practiced nurse, should go.

However, as soon as Sarah got into Joe's carriage, he turned and started profanely insulting Fred before applying the whip to his horse. After they traveled just out of sight, Fred heard his wife screaming in pain and terror. He ran to the spot, only to find Joe riding off and his wife lying on the ground, bloodied and beaten.

She told her husband that Joe started hurling insults about him, so she got out of his buggy. As she began to walk back to her home, Joe attacked her from behind. "She was struck several times, was hit with a rock, and was kicked," the *Journal-Miner* reported.

"Dr. Southworth was summoned from Prescott and he found a number of contusions on her back and limbs, and her lip was cut apparently from having been hit in the mouth." Additionally, there was an imprint of a heel on Sarah's neck.

It took two weeks for Sarah to recover sufficiently to travel to the preliminary hearing against Joe. Although he was initially charged with assault with intent to kill, the charge was reduced to aggravated battery—a felony carrying one to five years.

"No evidence whatever was introduced to link the alleged assault to any former trouble between [Fred] and [Joe], if any existed," the paper reported. Joe "did not take the stand in his own defense, and no evidence was introduced in his behalf." He paid the $1,000 bond and was released to await his trial in the Arizona Superior Court.

The public was outraged over news of the incident. Even if Joe had reason to be angry at Fred, beating his elderly wife because of it was heinous and despicable. However, before his trial date for aggravated battery arrived, Joe was shot in the shoulder by Sarah's hand.

That particular morning, Joe was on his way to Kirkland Valley and stopped in front of Sarah's house. When Sarah appeared at the door to see who had arrived, Joe yelled: "There you are you ——," the newspaper sheepishly printed. Joe then continued on his way. However, sometime during the two o'clock hour, he returned and, according to Sarah, stopped his buggy twenty feet from the front of the house and immediately started hurling more insults at her. In light of her beating, Sarah was scared.

Then, according to Sarah, Joe made the mistake of starting toward her. She grabbed a shotgun that she had placed by the side of the door. Before Joe's foot could touch the ground, she fired. The blast hit his right shoulder with such force that it threw him back into the seat. His horse, now panicked, charged for home. Before Joe got too far, Sarah was able to fire a second blast but missed. She then went to where her husband, Fred, was working in the mines and told him, in front of others, what had just transpired. "Ever since [Joe] Mackin beat me up, I have been afraid of him," she told the group.

Dr. McNally arrived from Prescott to treat Joe and found his patient in a dire state. It was hoped that Joe would survive, but on his third day at the hospital, he suddenly declined before passing away.

Joe had been a resident of the area for over twelve years, having come from New York City. At the time of his death, he worked for the Eleanor Placer Mining Company of French Gulch. A native of Ireland, he had arrived in the United States fifteen years prior. He was forty-two.

A coroner's inquest was held. It was a disconsolate affair. The newspaper described the scene.

> *The occasion was a solemn one, the presence of death seeming to hover over the* [entire proceeding.] [Sarah] *was in attendance with her husband and although from her testimony it was evident she felt justified in her act, she patently realized that the question of whether she would be exonerated or be forced to face trial before the courts, hung in the balance. The brother of the dead man was there through all the proceedings and it was a dramatic moment when the widow of* [Joe] *Mackin, bowed with grief, was brought in the room, accompanied by a woman friend carrying the baby who is not old enough to know of the tragic end of his father.*

The jury was taken to the Ruffner Funeral Parlor to view Joe's body. Seventeen wounds were shown, and Dr. McNally testified that the angle of the wounds was completely consistent with Sarah's story. He stated that "he removed pieces of clothing from the wounds, probed them, and staunched the flow of blood." In his opinion death was caused from shock, following the loss of blood. He further testified to conversations he had with Joe at his house and the hospital in which Joe stated he was "shot from a window in the Moses' house as he was driving by, and it was his impression that it was a woman that did the shooting, although he could not be sure." This was the first time Joe's story was publicized, and people were shocked and disbelieving.

The next witness to take the stand was Deputy Sheriff Joseph Young, "who professed to have had some experience with gunshot wounds," the paper related. He stated that, generally, wounds were smaller at the point of entrance and larger at the point of exit. He disagreed with the doctor, feeling that Joe was shot in the back.

The courtroom hushed when the most anticipated witness, Sarah, calmly took the stand. "Only once did she threaten to give way to emotion," the paper stated, "and that was when she was telling of the beating administered to her by [Joe] in the early part of September."

She then told her account of the fatal shooting as recorded by the paper:

> *On the morning of that day she was attending to her duties, at the moment being in the chicken yard when [Joe] came along in the horse and buggy. Spying her, he gave utterance to a vile epithet and drove on. In the afternoon she was in the kitchen and hearing a buggy stop she looked out of the door. It was [Joe] on his return journey from Kirkland. Seeing her, he started to get out of the buggy, at the same time saying ——— ——— ——— ——— and reaching for his right hip pocket. She picked up a shotgun, conveniently near, and blazed away. The load struck [Joe,] who had one foot on the buggy step, in the right shoulder and knocked him back on the seat. The horse, frightened by the noise of the gun, commenced to run, and as the buggy got in range within the house, she fired again, but missed the mark.*

When asked why she fired the second shot, Sarah said she did not know.

A tense moment occurred during Sarah's cross-examination, when defense attorney Joseph Morgan asked if she had ever threatened to kill Joe. She said no. Morgan pressed the question several times, and she continued to deny it. "Then she turned to Morgan and said: 'I think I know what you are trying to get at, Mr. Morgan,'" the paper recorded. "'After [Joe] was bound over to the Superior Court on the charge of assaulting me, I met you in the corridor and asked you what I should do if [Joe] assaulted me again. And what did you say?'"

"I told you to protect yourself," the lawyer was forced to admit.

Fred Moses followed his wife on the stand. According to the paper, he confirmed his wife's testimony about the assault and added that the following morning before sunrise, Joe had fired two rifle shots into the house. Fred then went outside, carefully stalking the culprit. He spied Joe on his horse and heard him say: "The ——— ——— won't put their heads out of the house tonight" before riding away. Later, in the light of day, Fred recovered the alleged shells. He "also swore that on several occasions [Joe] had threatened to kill him," although the reason why was not disclosed.

The wife of the dead man was called next, and "she claimed she was 75–100 yards away when [Joe and Sarah] came down the road in [Joe's] buggy and she saw Sarah get up in the buggy, attempt to strike her husband and fall out, alighting on her back," before she walked back home.

She further testified that her husband, after being shot, made it home "and was able to walk [into] the house unassisted." He told her that he did not know who fired the shot.

Then the brother of the deceased, Peter Mackin, testified that his brother "was wounded by unknown parties while riding past the Moses home" and "had done nothing to bring about the shooting."

That concluded the testimony. After deliberation, the jury found "that said Sarah Ann Moses fired said shot under the impression that her life was in danger; therefore we, the jury, find that Sarah Ann Moses was justified in her act," the paper declared.

But after the coroner's jury exonerated Sarah Moses, Joe's brother Peter felt that the ruling was unjust. What his dead brother had told him was at odds with Sarah's testimony, as was the deputy's judgment of where the buckshot entered. So, sometime during the earliest hours of the morning, he demanded a warrant be issued for Sarah Moses for murder. "Judge McLean refused to come downtown at that hour of the morning and also advised that the County Attorney be notified before such a step was taken," the paper reported. However, serendipitously, the justice of the peace was in his office signing "some important documents which had to be sent away" on the 3:00 a.m. train. Peter appeared before him and swore to the warrant.

Later that day, Sarah was arrested and released after a $1,000 bond was provided by two concerned citizens.

During Sarah's murder trial, "no new evidence of a material nature was forthcoming," the paper reported, "although the prosecution presented 12 witnesses who covered ground only of an incidental character bearing on the tragedy." The defense called seven witnesses. The only direct evidence of the shooting was given by Sarah, and her story was practically the same as that given during the coroner's investigation.

Evidence was introduced on behalf of Joe "to the effect that the deceased had made an oral statement that he was shot while passing by the Moses place, but did not know who fired the shots."

Judge J.M.W. Moore's decision was thoughtful, specific and mirrored public opinion:

> *Taking into consideration the evidence of Peter Mackin, the complaining witness, as to the elevation of the house occupied by Mrs. Moses, the roadway, and the position occupied by the buggy being driven by the deceased, the evidence of the attending physician as to the location of the wounds, I am convinced that the evidence of Mrs. Moses as to the position of the deceased when the shot was fired was as stated by her. That [Joe] Mackin was getting out of the buggy and was in such a position at that time that the shot took the direction as indicated by the attending physician—that there*

is no evidence of the shots being fired by anyone else than the defendant nor from any other point in the house.

Hence, the conclusion forces itself upon me that the statements made by [Sarah] Moses are true. The assault made upon [her] by [Joe] Mackin at a previous time, unprovoked and unreasonable, was brutal and has never been explained subsequent to the shooting. The condition of the body and mind of [Sarah] from the assault made upon her up to and at the time of the shooting, clearly shows she was in constant fear of her life and had reason to believe from what had transpired before and from the actions of [Joe] at the time of the shooting, that he intended to carry out his threats. That she was forced to protect herself I find her justified and order her discharged.

However, Peter Mackin still harbored his doubts about the killing. Was the doctor correct? Did Sarah shoot his brother in the front out of fear for her life? Or was the deputy sheriff correct in that she shot him in the back in retribution for the assault?

Picture of the Palace restaurant, year unknown. *Courtesy www.visitwhc.org.*

A group relaxing near Prescott. *Courtesy WikiMedia Commons.*

The following February, when a road was being surveyed that would go through the area where his brother was murdered, Peter compelled the county supervisors to authorize a survey "of certain lands and the location of buildings that figured in the shooting and killing of Joe Mackin late last year," according to the paper. This action was "for the purpose of perpetuating the evidence in case any new developments might arise."

None ever did, however, and the gun-toting granny lived out the rest of her days quietly.

10

THE DYNAMITE ATTACK ON J.S. ACKER

By Drew Desmond

For residents of Prescott today, J.S. Acker is remembered most warmly. Due to his philanthropy, the popular annual downtown music festival held during the holiday season is named in his honor. On his death, he willed to the city a popular park. However, at the time, Acker's bequest surprised many people.

For, while he was alive, most considered him to be a bit cranky and cantankerous. For example, when children entered his bookstore and candy shop, Acker required them to show that they had money to spend. If not, he forced them to leave. If one boy had money and his accompanying friend did not, only the one with the money was able to step inside.

So, when three dogs were found dead outside the Acker house, someone thought the worst—that Acker was purposely trying to kill the canines.

It all started with pesky rodents and a violent storm. J.S. Acker wanted to rid his house and outbuilding of the pests that were nesting there. He bought some cheese, put poison on it and set some around his property. It was a practice done "a great number of times in the past, and always, as this time, for the sole purpose of exterminating the rodents," Acker later stated.

During these times, Acker would keep his own dog inside so that she could not reach the poison. However, things went wrong when a violent storm blew down a section of Acker's fence, opening his yard to the neighbors' wandering pets. Unfortunately, three dogs entered, ate the cheese and died.

Scuttlebutt around town quickly exaggerated the facts of the incident and painted Acker as ruthless. The fallacious story grew into a belief that Acker's dog was in heat and Acker purposely opened the fence to allow any male dog within. Then, it was rumored, he placed the poisonous cheese just outside his own dog's reach for the males to consume. Exaggerations swirled that, instead of three, the old coot employed this method to kill nineteen dogs!

Then, in the still of the night on April 21, 1917, someone tried to throw a stick of dynamite through Acker's parlor window. Fortunately, the incendiary did not crash through the pane but fell below it before exploding.

"By a miracle no one was hurt," the *Journal-Miner* exclaimed. The blast shattered the windows of nearby houses and "was plainly heard all over the town." Mr. and Mrs. Acker were awakened by the blast, and they immediately telephoned the sheriff's office.

"From the appearance of the place it was evident that someone passed the house and threw a stick of giant powder, to which was attached a lighted fuse," the paper reported. "The missile struck just below the parlor window and when it exploded tore a large hole in the ground at that point, ripped loose all the boards at the north end of the house and shattered every pane of glass in the parlor windows, the concussion also breaking and cracking windows in other parts of the residence."

The next morning, Acker told the newspaper that he was baffled and perplexed by the attack and had no idea who the culprit might be.

Acker should have felt fortunate. It was determined that had the dynamite gone through the parlor window it could have brought the entire wood structure down with the Ackers still in it. As it was, the explosion occurred near the foundation of the house, blasting a large pile of dirt that stretched across the public sidewalk.

When no witnesses could be found for several days, Acker personally offered a reward of $500 for the capture of those responsible. The Yavapai County Board of Supervisors quickly matched the amount, making the total reward a hefty $1,000, or about five months' pay for the average man.

The investigation seemed promising at first but quickly went cold. "The sheriff's office continued...trying to get together facts in connection with the outrage, but was unable to locate anything on which a case might be hung," the paper reported. "Several warm clues were followed, [but] there were no witnesses to the deed, and it [was] difficult to gather any coherent accounts."

When the rumors of the nineteen dead dogs finally reached Acker, he was flabbergasted. He immediately felt compelled to write the

The old county jail building on the Plaza, early 1900s. *Courtesy Sharlot Hall Museum.*

newspaper to quell the gossip: "I learned today for the first time that there is a persistent rumor in the city to the effect that I had tied my female dog in my front yard for the purpose of attracting other dogs, and had deliberately scattered poison…out of her reach…and had, in this manner, killed…19 dogs."

After revealing what really happened, Acker continued: "I…state positively that if any dog was poisoned on my premises that it was wholly an accident and without design or intention on my part, and furthermore that I am an owner and admirer of dogs, and would be the last person in the world to cause the death of anyone's dog by poison."

While considering the evidence, some wondered whether the dynamite was thrown at the large parlor window and fell to the ground or was purposefully placed at the foundation. The difference was key to the motive—a warning, or an intention to maim or murder.

However, it should be noted that by all accounts not only were Mr. and Mrs. Acker awakened by the blast, but more significantly, so also was Acker's dog. It seems that if someone had made the sound of opening the front gate in the middle of the night and started skulking under the parlor window, nearly every canine created would have a conniption, barking alarmingly and incessantly. Yet, this did not occur. Therefore, it is far more likely that the dynamite was thrown and that the intention was for more than a warning.

In any event, Acker's cooling explanation in conjunction with the heat of the law stopped any further attempts at revenge.

Despite the rich reward, the culprit was never captured, and the incident eventually fell into obscurity.

11

RICH RANCHMAN TRIES TO GET AWAY WITH IT

By Drew Desmond

To most observers in 1918, it seemed that the Stephens ranching family was traveling through life aboard a luxury yacht. The average worker would have to toil for 130 years to earn the net worth of the patriarch, Joe Stephens.

However, below the placid surface lay the ugly encrusted barnacles of dysfunction, discord and discontent that would soon see the light of day. For it was the cold-blooded, broad-daylight murder of a popular ranch hand by the son, Harry "Bud" Stephens, that would capsize the family's reputation.

Joe's wife, May, was younger than her husband and enjoyed the material things in life but had to endure a hefty cost to obtain them. Despite Arizona's alcohol prohibition, Joe was known for frequent drunken tirades often directed toward his spouse, making her life miserable.

Joe adored his twenty-two-year-old son but raised him to become a spoiled, sophomoric, yes-man to his father.

Enter the ranch hand, thirty-six-year-old Robert J. "Bob" Miller, a chiseled, kindly, ladies' man who worked at the Stephens cattle empire. The unmarried Miller had no known family. At his funeral, the newspaper observed that despite the fact that no relatives could be located, there was still a large crowd with "the larger part of the gathering being composed of women."

May Stephens, forty-five, would occasionally do the cooking at some of the chuck wagons on the ranch, and she must have met Bob there. To him, she was a damsel in distress. She must have been flattered and enthralled by the attentions of a kind, attractive man nine years her junior.

They grew close as they talked, with Robert counseling the haggard wife to leave her husband. He promised that he would go with her and rescue her from her anguished life. She acquiesced. A day was set, and plans were made, but her husband and son got word of the scheme and vowed to ambush it.

Robert recruited the help of Sid Marks and Ernest Marlow, and together, the four left for Prescott in Ernest's automobile. When they got to a point near the summit, Joe and Bud Stephens overtook them and demanded that they stop or Joe and Bud would shoot them. The *Weekly Journal-Miner* described the scene:

Bud jumped out of the car and yelled at his mother: "What the hell are you doing here?"

"A stream of profanity and obscene talk [was] directed toward the woman by her husband," the paper reported as "Bud echoed the vulgar language his father used." Sheepish to print such language in 1918, the paper reported that Joe told his wife, "If you go with that man, you're no better than a ———— w ———!" (Perhaps "god-damned whore"?)

May told Bud and Joe that she never had relations with Bob. Joe replied, "You know you have," a judgment parroted by the son to his mother's face.

May then whispered to Ernest that she was afraid of her husband and son. "Then father and son made an attempt to pull [May] out of the car. They tore several buttons off her garments" in the attempt. May protested that she did not want to leave the car. She told Sid Marks: "I don't want to ride with them. They are both drunk and they might kill me."

The situation stalemated. As Joe and Bud left, the husband vowed that "they would go to town and get a gun and shoot the whole damn bunch of [them]."

To avoid such a confrontation, the car detoured over a rough backroad to Jerome Junction. It took them until 3:30 a.m. to roll into Prescott. May asked Bob to get her a room, and the two left the car at Gurley and Granite Streets to lodge the lady at the Golden Eagle Hotel.

The next morning, Bud Stephens was found crying. When asked what was the matter, Bud replied "that a man had broke up his home and his paw and maw had split up and now all he could do was to leave the country," the *Miner* reported.

Later that morning, an acquaintance, John Vickers, found Bud at the Palace Saloon crying, "nervous, and very much upset." John accompanied Bud to the Reif Hotel and found Ernest and Sid staying there. Bud went ahead to the room, and by the time John caught up, "Bud was leaning on the bed and had hold of [Ernest]. Bud said, 'Tell me where she is or I'll bust you.'" Then Bud hit Ernest in the face, cutting his eye.

Bob, Ernest and Sid were quickly rounded up and put in jail. After learning that May was in room 4 at the Golden Eagle, an undersheriff was sent to investigate. He would eventually testify that he found May in possession of her jewelry and money, "but she would not go back to the Stephens' ranch."

The sheriff himself would later testify that he went to visit May in the early afternoon to confirm her story. She told the sheriff that he had "no right to hold those boys in jail." The sheriff explained to her "that she had been reported as missing with a lot of jewelry and money" and that he had to hold them until he was sure she had not been robbed.

May reiterated to the sheriff that she wasn't going back to her husband. Instead, she was "going to get a divorce and would never have anything to do with her husband again." When the sheriff asked why she was unwilling to go back, May quipped that "it was a perfect hell."

The sheriff related this news to Joe and Bud. He then went to the jail to release the three men and told Bob, "Mr. Stephens tells me Bud wants to get his mother back to the ranch. Now if you will keep out of sight until things blow over, everything will be all right."

However, Bob refused, insisting "that he had done nothing to hide out for." Meanwhile, both father and son tried their best to get the wife and mother to come back home. She only refused.

Bud, entirely distraught at this point, headed to Hill's Hardware and bought himself a Colt .38. On leaving, he spotted Bob across the Plaza on Gurley Street.

According to the paper, Robert had bought a suit at Bruchman's clothing store and went to pick it up. As he began to leave, Bud walked in. They passed each other when Bud "suddenly turned and fired into [Bob's] back with [his] Colt .38." Bob turned "so that he faced [Bud] and began to crumple before he dropped to the floor." Bud fired two more shots, which left Bob prostrate, face-down. Then Bud "continued to pump lead into the man's back until his gun was emptied."

As the shooting started, Joe was heard to say, "Stay with the son-of-a-bitch!" Bud then stepped out the door, and his father encouraged him, yelling in a loud voice: "Keep shooting, kid, god dammit, keep shooting!" Bud took time to reload and fired two more bullets into Bob before the body lay limp. Then his father called out, asking, "Did you get the dirty...?" (the paper only offered blank lines). He then leaned over and told his son: "Well,

Portrait of Sam Hill, owner of
Sam Hill Hardware. *Courtesy*
www.visitwhc.org.

this son-of-a-bitch got exactly what was coming to him.—Come on Bud,
let's go over to the sheriff's office." Bud turned himself in and was booked
for murder.

In speaking of the killing the next day, the paper reported that May said:
"I am to blame—No, not me. It was that god-damned son of a bitch, Joe
Stephens." She then told a friend "that [Bob] was a gentleman in every way
and also that she was going to get a divorce from her husband."

The trial, the first ever heard in the current Yavapai County Courthouse,
was a salacious "crime of the century" that gained more coverage in the
newspaper than the concurrent closing days of World War I.

"This sensational homicide case is attracting quite a large crowd to the
courtroom," the paper reported, "and standing room was at a premium.
The bailiff was kept busy shooing people away who persisted in blocking
up the main entrance to the place." Most of the audience in the three rows
of seating were women. There were sixty-eight members of the fairer sex
jammed into the courtroom at one point.

The courthouse's first murder trial would also pit two of Yavapai
County's best attorneys against each other. Joe Stephens hired P.W.
O'Sullivan, while the county attorney tapped E.S. Clark to be special
deputy prosecutor.

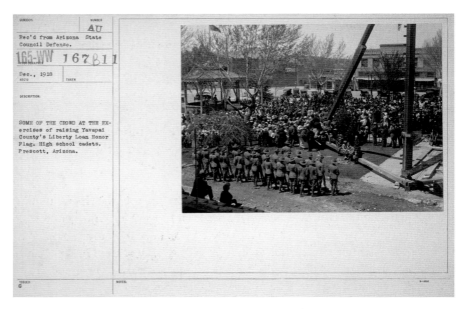

Raising the Liberty Loan Honor Flag at the Plaza in 1918. *Courtesy WikiMedia Commons.*

O'Sullivan described the defense's case in his opening statement: "This defendant was temporarily insane at the time he killed Bob Miller....Miller, you must remember, had been paying attentions to [May] for many months, and so bold had become his conduct that his actions were exciting the comment not only of the friends and neighbors, but also the other members of the family as well."

"At the time of the homicide," he continued, "young Bud was in the heat of passion, sick at heart and distressed, and when he met [Bob] on the fatal afternoon he shot the man before he had time to collect his wits and cool down a bit."

O'Sullivan also took the opportunity to impugn the character of the deceased: Bob "had an unenviable record in his home state of Idaho....He had seduced a girl and had to skip out of the state...."

On the stand, Joe admitted that he employed Bob at his ranch. "That didn't hurt him as a worker," Joe said.

Attorney E.S. Clark reminded Joe about an instance a year prior when Joe found May "cooking for some of the boys." The attorney asked:

> *"You testified that you didn't like to have* [May] *paying more attention to* [Bob] *Miller than to you, Did you not?"*

"I don't think I said that," was the reply.
"You must of thought that [May] *was infatuated with* [Bob] *at the time."*
"I don't know. I thought [Bob] *was infatuated with her."*
"You continued to think so?"
"I think so yet."

Joe further testified that he had visited his wife the morning of the killing to get her to come home. "I know I haven't treated you right," he told her, "we know what [Bob] has done to you. We know it all."

But she replied, "No, I've quit you for good."

Sheriff Joe Young's testimony revealed that Bob had told the sheriff that he had spent the night at the St. Michael Annex Hotel. However, "inquiry there... had brought out the fact that the landlady...had not rented any rooms" that night. Young further testified that when he visited May at the Golden Eagle, he told her that her husband and son were willing to forgive everything.

"THEY would forgive HER?" Clark asked in disbelief.

"Yes," was the sheriff's reply.

When Sid Marks testified about the incident of Joe and Bud stopping Ernest's car, Joe lost control. Sid said that, after May denied infidelity, Bud told his mother, "You know you have." Joe burst out: "That's a god-damned lie!" He was immediately cited as being in contempt of court and spent the rest of the afternoon in jail.

The defendant, Bud, then took the stand. Trying to grasp at a temporary insanity defense, Bud testified that "he had but faint recollection of the affair, that he was terribly remorseful for what he had done, but that he believed that killing Bob was the only thing which could prevent a break-up of the home."

"During the time [Bud] was being examined by his counsel, he retained his composure to a wonderful degree, answering all questions put to him in a firm tone and telling a story which was calculated to go straight to the hearts of the listening jurymen," the paper observed. "But at the close of the session, after he had been under the grilling fire of the cross-examination of Special Prosecutor E.S. Clark, he left the witness box in a highly nervous state, and during the last hour of the cross-examination seemed to have not a little difficulty extracting himself from the verbal pitfalls into which the prosecutor led him."

Under the tough cross-examination, Bud was forced to admit "that the domestic felicity of the Stephens home was not the best in the world and that as a matter of fact much wrangling had taken place there between...his parents." The boy was also forced to admit on the stand that "drunkenness was no uncommon thing at the Stephens' ranch."

Then May took the stand. Within a week of Bob's death, she had moved back into the Stephens home. She now told a tale of household perfection—even after Bud's admissions to the contrary. There had been no drinking, swearing or quarrels ever, according to her now.

She now claimed that Bob was trying to steal her away, that he planned to take her to Idaho via the 11:00 a.m. train and elope with her.

When cross-examined, E.S. Clark tested her as to why she did not tell this to anyone sooner:

> *"Was it not because in your maternal devotion to Bud you were willing to sacrifice yourself, even to the extent of losing your good name?"*
>
> *"No. It was because I considered that I had it coming to me."*
>
> *"You were entirely willing, were you not, to let him use you as an excuse for his killing of* [Bob]*?"*
>
> *There was no answer.*
>
> *"You were willing to tell any story, were you not, even though it blackened your reputation, if it helped him escape punishment?"*
>
> *Again there was no answer.*
>
> *"Did you ever imagine prior to this killing that your husband and son would be willing to sacrifice your reputation to save themselves?"*
>
> *"I did not."*
>
> *Did you not say…that when* [Joe] *was abusing you and using vile language, that* [Bob] *had taken your part?"*
>
> *She denied saying it.*
>
> *"Do you remember how, when your husband told you about the girl Bob was implicated in Idaho, you said that Bob was a better man than he even at that?"*
>
> *She replied that she didn't mean it.*

It seemed obvious that May had been completely sucked back into her "perfect hell."

Then Special Prosecutor Clark called a surprise witness. It was none other than the highly respected former Yavapai County sheriff, George Ruffner. He testified that Bud threatened to kill Bob the Monday prior. "'I am going to kill Miller,' said Bud to me after we were seated at the table. I told the boy that he would have to cut out such rough talk while he was around me, and upon his refusal to cease making such remarks, I got up and left the place, as I did not want to listen to anymore such talk."

Ruffner dropped another bombshell when he testified that father Joe confided in him that he "believed there was nothing wrong between his wife and Bob because [May] had been without passion of any sort since the birth of her son 22 years ago."

In closing arguments, prosecution pointed out the discrepancies in the testimony between the Stephens family and law enforcement officers. Defense promised that if Bud were "acquitted, he will enter the army and will there get the discipline which has been so sadly lacking in his life up to the present time."

"Gentlemen of the jury," O'Sullivan said, "let this boy go free so that any sins which may be charged against him may be vindicated on the battlefields of France."

The jurors received their instructions and retired. It took two ballots to find Bud guilty and two ballots to sentence him to life. The entire exercise took them less than a half hour.

When the verdict was delivered, Bud was stunned and showed extreme nervousness. When he first faced the bars of the jail, tears began to stream down his face. But Bud's father would make sure that he wouldn't stay there long.

In his closing argument, E.S. Clark prognosticated that Bud "probably reasoned that in the event he was convicted...and by reason of his father's wealth and power...he would appeal the case and fight off the execution of the court's sentence until such time as the war would be over and then he would not have to go." This is precisely what happened.

More than that, O'Sullivan got a new trial due to the fact that jury instructions did not include the possibility of a second-degree murder charge. Further, jurisdiction was moved to Coconino County and Flagstaff. Bud was allowed out on the appeal and a hefty $50,000 bail.

In the second trial, there were no surprises, and O'Sullivan was ready. It took the jury just forty-five minutes to find Bud not guilty. "Pray God! Oh! My boy!" Joe exclaimed.

Things could not have gone better for Bud. Yes, there was the embarrassment and cost of the trial, but Bud spent nearly the entire time out on bail. Additionally, as his trial dragged on, he missed being drafted into World War I. With his cold-blooded murder of Bob Miller, Bud Stephens successfully obtained all the results his little heart desired.

Eventually, May did leave Joe and married a man named Calhoun. She died in 1937 at age fifty-eight. Joe eventually became a resident of the Arizona Pioneers' Home until his death in 1948 at age eighty-two. When a reporter interviewed him there about his pioneering past, Joe made absolutely no mention of his former wife or his son Bud.

12

MURDER PLOT AT THE PIONEERS' HOME

By Drew Desmond

For attorney A.G. Baker, it seemed a routine chore. He had made out several wills and testaments before; the only difference this time was that the elderly client requested that the lawyer come down to the street and meet him in a car for the signing.

Baker left his office with two copies of the will in hand to be signed by a paralytic Arizona Pioneers' Home resident, William Debus. It would leave nurse Clarance Dyer all of Debus's worldly possessions on his death. It was Dyer who accompanied the elderly man to Baker's office. When the wills were presented to the client, he signed them by making an "X" with his left hand. "The document was witnessed by Baker and…the legal work [was paid for] with two $5 bills," the *Weekly Journal-Miner* reported.

It was at that moment that undersheriff Ed Bowers suddenly charged to the vehicle and leveled a large six-shooter directly at the aged man's chest. "Throw up your hands!" Bowers demanded.

Clarance Dyer, the would-be beneficiary, was a new employee at the Arizona Pioneers' Home. He had been a stateside army nurse and had been drafted into the service during World War I. The reason for Dyer's arrival was the Spanish influenza pandemic and the resulting fatal pneumonia. The last quarter of 1918 alone brought over two thousand deaths to Arizona from the malady.

It took the quarantining of whole towns and the cancellations of public events before the disease was arrested. Of course, healthcare workers enjoyed

The historic Old Governor's Mansion. *Courtesy WikiMedia Commons.*

no such precaution, and fatalities in that field were particularly acute. As a result, the army released a number of its nurses and orderlies to finish their service by working in state facilities that were suffering from manpower shortages. Dyer was a part of this program.

He enjoyed his new job and the unique facility that employed him. He did his work well and seemed to get along with both the residents and his coworkers, one of whom was named Carrier Thompson.

Thompson was thought of highly. The home's superintendent described him as "an extremely efficient nurse and, in fact, knew nearly as well as a doctor would, how to take care of people."

Thompson quickly befriended Dyer, but their conversations soon turned nefarious. First, they concocted a scheme to take some army-issued blankets that a resident owned. They would store them in Dyer's quarters, sell them and split the profit. They thought that since Dyer had just come from the army he could provide a plausible explanation if they were found.

However, before they could carry out their plot, the blankets were moved to a secure location. So, the pair turned their attention to a different prize. This time, it involved the emptying of a recently deceased resident's bank account by forging a check. However, this plan failed as well, as the bank became suspicious, held the check and did not honor it. Despite their unfortunate luck, the two would not be dissuaded from taking the easy money that crime could bring and plotted an even larger haul.

It was Thompson, as usual, who hatched the scheme. He knew that one of the residents, William Debus, had the equivalent of eighteen months' pay squirreled away in the bank. Thompson's plan was to forge a will, giving the estate to Dyer. Then Thompson would poison Debus, and the two malfeasants would split the estate.

Their first plot involved petty theft, the second forgery and fraud. Now they were planning premeditated murder, and the implications caused them to begin to act suspiciously.

Soon, county attorney Neil Clark was made aware of the situation, and he came up with his own trap. First, he secretly made a thorough three-hour search of Thompson's quarters, which revealed several stolen items but no poison. To be safe, "Clark also made preparations through local officials to keep track of any poison that might be sold during the week in the Prescott drugstores," the paper revealed.

Debus himself was kept in the dark about the matter "for the reason that it was thought a shock of this sort might be fatal to the bed-ridden patient." Yet, Debus had already become "suspicious of Thompson lately and that he had worried considerably and was at the point of asking for protection, when the trap was sprung," the paper reported.

It was Dyer who accompanied the man claiming to be Debus to Baker's office for the signing of the will. So, when Undersheriff Bowers told the old man to throw up his hands, he knew the man could do so despite his claim of paralysis. Bowers knew he was pointing his gun at Thompson.

A subsequent search of Thompson's quarters revealed a "60cc bottle three-quarters full of Chlorodyne pills," it was reported. This was the poison Thompson intended to use.

Informed of Thompson's arrest, Debus was "relieved and very cheerful. 'I feel better than I have for weeks and I intend to live a long time,'" he was reported to say.

To his credit, Thompson always stuck with the story he told police immediately after he was arrested, although it proved to be utterly implausible. He blamed Dyer, stating that Dyer had gotten a woman pregnant and in order to marry her had to prove to her family that he had some means to support her. Thompson stated that Dyer approached him with the idea of forging the will, showing it to the girl's family and then burning it. At trial, Thompson's story was corroborated by no one.

Dyer's account, however, was corroborated by the superintendent of the Arizona Pioneers' Home, law enforcement and the county attorney's office itself. For the man Thompson trusted was, in fact, informing authorities from

The keys used for the cells at the old Yavapai County Jail. *Courtesy www.visitwhc.org.*

the start! It was Dyer who informed his superintendent about the blankets, the check and the murder plot.

It did not take the jury long to find Thompson guilty. Although he won a chance at a retrial, the testimony and the outcome remained the same.

"Realizing his ambition to work in state institutions," the newspaper quipped, "Carrier Thompson [was] left in charge of Sheriff Warren Dais for Florence, where he will serve a term…of 10–14 years."

Thompson would never be heard from again in Prescott. Dyer decided to become a permanent resident of the city and continued his profession as a well-respected and highly trusted caregiver.

13

SHOT THE MESSENGER

By Drew Desmond

t was December 23, 1920. Mr. and Mrs. Frank Olzer were sitting below their room in the Reif Hotel eating dinner at the Hoffman Grill, when one of Mr. Olzer's employees, John Lohlein, entered the establishment in a terrible plight. His face and coat were soaked in blood, and he was clearly inebriated.

"Why, what's the matter with you?" Mrs. Olzer exclaimed. "There is blood all over you!"

The couple supposed that Lohlein had been fighting. He was excited but initially offered no clue as to what had happened. They convinced him to go upstairs and wash the bloodstains from his face and coat. Frank Olzer soon followed and noticed that Lohlein had a gun in his possession and attempted to talk him into surrendering it. "Give me that gun," Olzer said.

"I killed one man tonight and I would just as soon kill another," Lohlein replied. Olzer protested that surely Lohlein hadn't killed anyone, but the blood-covered man was insistent. "I killed a man and hid him behind a bush," Lohlein stated, "but I won't tell you who he is. Wait until tomorrow and you will know. I killed the wrong man, and I'm going to kill three more men and then kill myself."

Although astonished, Olzer still was not convinced and advised Lohlein to go home and go to bed. Lohlein began to weep. He stated that the man he had killed had said something derogatory concerning Mayde Hayden, a woman he was living with, and that he couldn't stand it. He further revealed that the body could be found behind a clump of bushes about seven miles north of Prescott on the Ash Fork Road.

Having sent Lohlein home, Frank Olzer talked the matter over with his wife as to whether they should report Lohlein's story to the police. After going to the Palace for a late light meal, they decided to go to the sheriff's office. Even if Lohlein's story was untrue, they were still concerned he might hurt himself. They walked to the sheriff's office, met with Deputy Joe Cook and told him the story.

"How John Lohlein ran the gauntlet of city police before there was the slightest suspicion that he would soon be under arrest for murder," the newspaper reported, "is the whimsicalist [*sic*] angle of the sensational developments of [this case.]"

First, two women from his boardinghouse called police to report Lohlein drunk and carrying firearms. One of these women was the lady in the case, Mayde Hayden. She and a friend, a Mrs. Hawthorne, along with Officer Richard Twamley, were able to talk Lohlein out of two revolvers.

At this point, Lohlein somehow misplaced his key and couldn't enter his boardinghouse, so he walked about downtown. A "service car driver"

Counter at the Palace restaurant, year unknown. *Courtesy www.visitwhc.org.*

noticed him "drunk and packing a big roll of money," the paper described. The driver informed another officer, who talked with Lohlein "to ascertain the degree of his inebriation and satisfied that the man was able to take care of himself and his money, let him go."

It was after this incident, around 9:00 p.m., when the Olzers related Lohlein's account to Deputy Cook, who immediately sent Deputies Warren Davis and Joseph Furst to Lohlein's boardinghouse at 130 North Montezuma Street. They found him sitting on the porch, unable to get inside.

"You have killed a man," Davis said gravely. Lohlein collapsed, "breaking down but not admitting anything" except that "he had been out that way," the paper reported.

Officers searched Lohlein's room and found "an overcoat, stiffened with blood despite the fact that it had been washed." More blood was found on his clothing. "Examination of the car, which was driven back to Prescott and run into Lohlein's garage, revealed beside a bullet hole, a quantity of blood on the front seat, and on the running board," the paper reported. There was no evidence of a scuffle.

Immediately, law officers traveled to the reported location of the body. The officers began searching the area with flashlights and soon found a trail of blood and tracks in the snow. "The slayer had evidently been either drunk or so frightened that he had dragged [the body] through a stretch of snow instead of over the hard ground at one side," the paper described. "The snow on the edge of the road was slightly trampled showing the attempts of the man to take hold of the body and drag it to the hiding."

The body was left between the Dolly Ranch and the Prescott Gun Club's target range. There, just as had been described by Lohlein, they found the remains of Charles Summers lying face-down in this snow. His clothes and face were covered with blood. A bullet hole in the top of his head was clotted and sticky. A pearl-handled pocketknife was lying on his stomach. Nearby was a wallet containing only a certificate of registration. Every pocket on his person had been rummaged with the linings pulled out. Only a nickel and a nickel-plated watch were found in his brand-new coat.

"The body had been dragged fully 66 feet from the road," the paper related. "No empty shells were to be found near the spot." His hat, found by the roadside, was "filled with blood and brain tissue."

About midnight, the officers returned to the scene of the homicide with the coroner and a jury. They also brought with them Lohlein's shoes, which "fitted exactly the tracks at the road's edge and where the body was left," the paper reported.

The coroner's jury found that the bullet that ended Summers's life entered his right cheek, exited through the top of his head at the back and continued through the roof of the car just above the passenger seat.

Later, when Lester Ruffner examined the body at his funeral home, he found "a second entrance wound occurring in the head over the left eye and passing downward. No exit wound was found....The second shot crossed the path of the first, obstructing it with a piece or pieces of fractured bone, making it impossible to probe the wound from the left cheek to the back of the head," the paper reported.

After reviewing Summers's body and the evidence around the scene, the corner's jury found that Summers came to his death by gunshot wounds inflicted by Lohlein.

Summers, aged fifty-one or fifty-two, was raised in Wyoming, was unmarried and was for a number of years in the employee of W.M. Coburn. Eight years earlier, Summers had come to Arizona to work on Coburn's ranch at Globe. Most recently, he had been cattle inspector for Yavapai County. Although he occasionally drank, he was not known to be quarrelsome.

John Lohlein was a saddler employed at Frank Olzer's Arizona Saddlery Shop on North Cortez Street. He reportedly had a wife and two children living in Los Angeles and a brother who lived in the local area.

The accused was taken to the city garage, where his automobile, "still bearing the splotches of blood and cerebral tissues from the head of the deceased," had been moved from the rear of Lohlein's boardinghouse. Standing there, looking at the gory traces of the act, Lohlein maintained his coolness for only a few moments. Then, sinking down, he nearly collapsed onto the floor but was pinned between two automobiles parked close together. He caught himself and sat down on the running board of one of the cars and began to tell Officers Davis and Furst his account of the homicide.

He expressed no regrets or horror but admitted that both he and Summers were intoxicated and that he had suspected Summers of hostile motives when he reached for his pocket during an argument over some gossip concerning Hayden.

"I told him to take it back and he said he would not take anything back. I insisted and he reached for his gun and I shot him," Lohlein confessed.

In the course of his conversation with Davis and Furst, Lohlein "reviewed with some attention to detail, the incidents of the day that led up to the homicide," the paper reported. He said Summers and he were acquainted and that in the afternoon Summers had visited him at his workbench at the Arizona Saddlery company.

Another man entered whom Summers had borrowed money from in the past, and Summers was happy to show him a roll of bills totaling $200 (about three weeks' pay for the average man). Summers proudly stated that he had no reason to borrow any money now.

Lohlein related that both men traveled north on the Ash Fork Road and had been drinking when "remarks about [Hayden's] reputation, heard by her lover through the red haze of intoxication…caused the killing of Charles Summers," the paper concluded.

"Why, then, did you rob him?" Lohlein was asked.

"If I did that, I don't remember it," he replied. He could not account for the money found on his person. A pearl-handled Colt .45, found in Lohlein's car trunk, was believed to have belonged to Summers, who had an empty holster on his body when it was discovered. A half-pint bottle, about two-thirds filled with white mule, was also found on the accused at the time of his arrest.

John Lohlein was charged with murder in the first degree and held without bond awaiting trial.

"All during the trial the courtroom [was] crowded with people listening carefully for the details of the murder and its motives," the paper reported. The two most important witnesses were Frank Olzer, Lohlein's employer who saw him when he came into the Hoffman Grill, and Lohlein's lover, Mayde Hayden.

Olzer stated that Lohlein and Summers had been talking in his saddlery shop the day of the shooting and left the place together about 4:00 p.m. Olzer testified that he did not see the defendant again until he entered the Hoffman Grill in a sorry state around 7:00 p.m. Olzer then related, for the record, the account he and his wife gave police that fateful night.

As others testified, the story began to become clear to the courtroom observers. As Lohlein and Summers were talking in the saddlery, Summers meant to offer his companion some friendly advice. He said that people were describing Hayden as a loose woman and "going about the streets with everyone." Lohlein was incensed by the remark but kept his cool at the time.

After leaving the saddlery, the two men drove to Togo's Soft Drink and Cigar Shop on West Gurley near Granite Street to purchase, under the counter, a prohibited pint of white mule. They then traveled north out of town and began to celebrate some bottled fellowship. However, Lohlein kept thinking about the remark made about his lover and eventually demanded that Summers take it back.

"It was the warning of a friend who wanted to tell what other men were saying about the woman and advise him as to what he should best do," the paper related. When Summers protested that he was merely repeating what he had heard from others and would not take it back, Lohlein shot him twice before he hid the body.

Hayden testified for the defense, arguing that Lohlein had been in the midst of suffering from "alcoholic tremens." On cross-examination, the county attorney declined to question Hayden about the matter of prostitution and instead focused on her bias. It was revealed that she and Lohlein "had lived together for sometime, [and] that Lohlein had given her money continually," the paper noted.

Lohlein's story changed slightly when he testified on his own behalf. He explained that "he and Summers were riding in an automobile, had quarreled over a reference to Hayden, and that he challenged Summers to a fight. Lohlein stated that he had meant a fair fist-fight, but that Summers reached for his gun and boasted of his kills," the paper reported.

It took the jury twenty-four hours to reach a verdict. "Attaches and individuals drain[ed] into the room from everywhere," the paper described. The defendant was escorted by two deputy sheriffs and his attorneys.

"Lohlein sat rather slumped...and his face betrayed that he had passed a poor night," the paper observed. "His eyes darted a wordless question at the 12 jurors who filed into the room from the main doorway."

The Old (second) Yavapai County Courthouse, with the jail building to the right. *Courtesy Sharlot Hall Museum.*

There was complete silence as the jury's verdict was read. Lohlein's face contorted when it was announced that he was found guilty of murder in the second degree. A reporter stated that "it was impossible to tell whether it was relief or disappointment" on Lohlein's face.

He was later sentenced to twenty to thirty years in the Florence prison.

For the county attorney, there was still one aspect of the case that needed to be addressed: the bootleg liquor.

Just a week after Lohlein's sentencing, Mr. Togo and his wife, Annie Meyers, went on trial for selling the prohibited libation to Lohlein and Summers. Testifying in their own defense, both flatly denied the charge and remained composed and cool under cross-examination.

Then a parade of some of the most prominent men of the city testified to the defendants' sterling character. These included "bankers, lawyers, railroad officials, club leaders, mayors, and former mayors," the paper declared. Undoubtedly, all were customers of Togo's Soft Drink and Cigar Shop in one way or another.

Against this, the state was able to muster only the testimony of the convicted murderer Lohlein.

It didn't take long for the superior court jury to set Togo and his wife free. Perhaps they, too, were Togo's customers.

14

THE CHRISTMAS BUTCHER

By Drew Desmond

T was the night after Christmas 1920, and Frank Legrange was stirring about busily. He was planning to move away soon, and his list of chores seemed to be growing longer. For now, although the sun had already set, the rancher still had some butchering to do that simply couldn't wait. There would be even more chores to do tomorrow.

Another high priority on Legrange's to-do list was to clear out any evidence of his illegal moonshining operation. Legrange's bootlegging partner was a friend and neighbor named Walter Steinbrook, who gave word to Legrange that he was headed to South America in hopes of finding gold.

When friends came by a few days later to offer their well-wishes to Legrange and his wife, they noticed several small fires on the property emitting a unique odor. Legrange explained to them that he was burning up the used mash from the illegal still. In a few days, he told them, he and his wife would be moving to Mexico.

A couple of months after their departure, a miner was prospecting around the old Lagrange ranch and sniffed a disturbing odor coming from an abandoned mine shaft. Too spooked to investigate it himself, he decided to report it to the sheriff's office instead. However, the authorities did not find the miner's story compelling enough to investigate further.

Meanwhile, Steinbrook's nephew Frank Wilson had grown concerned about his uncle. Steinbrook told his family that he would be selling his mines and property and moving to California shortly after Christmas.

Steinbrook was a frequent letter writer, but neither friend nor family had gotten a single correspondence since he had departed. There had been no activity with his bank account, and people who owed him money began to wonder where to send it.

Months passed, and the weather became seasonably warmer, when Wilson heard the story of the miner being turned away from a ghastly smelling mine shaft. He convinced the deputy of Mayer, Arizona, Tommy Thompson, to join him in investigating the old Lagrange place for signs of Steinbrook.

By sighting the surrounding buzzards, it was fairly easy for the pair to locate the shaft. At its entrance was a swarm of flies and the smell of death. Gasping and choking, the pair reached the bottom of the shaft, where they found a large, tied canvas sack. The two withdrew, and a coroner's jury was called to investigate. The sack was recovered and brought unopened to Prescott for the inquiry.

The putrid smell was overwhelming when the sack was finally opened. Inside was one of the most gruesome sights ever recorded in Yavapai County history. One by one, portions of a decaying human body were revealed: "the head, the right side of the torso, the upper half of the left leg, the lower half of the left arm, a part of the spinal column, and the pelvis. Only the scalp, with a little reddish brown hair on it, and two lower left molars remained as possible clues to the identity of the man who had been murdered," the *Journal-Miner* detailed. The body had been mutilated beyond recognition, and no one had any idea as to the hiding place of the other body parts.

A hole in the skull, apparently from a large-caliber bullet, confirmed a murder. Additionally, a number of the teeth were missing. It was immediately thought to be the body of Steinbrook. His dentist was called to try to identify the skull as Steinbrook's, but the teeth that he had worked on happened to be the ones that were missing.

Assuming that the remains were those of his uncle, Wilson gave his opinion to the jury that the probable motive of the murder was robbery. His uncle was known to carry cash with him. This time, it was believed that he had $1,000—an average man's annual income—on his person.

A $1,000 reward was offered for the killer—$500 from Yavapai County and $500 from Wilson and the rest of Steinbrook's heirs.

The *Arizona Republic* wrote: "The slaying of Walter Steinbrook…is regarded by Yavapai County peace officers as the most brutal murder in a community where history has been written with the blood of homicide victims. Steinbrook's body had been literally butchered by the perpetrators of the crime. It had been hacked and hewn to bits, supposedly by an ax, though the death instrument was never found."

Immediately, suspicion fell on Lagrange. He was the last person to see the victim. Before Lagrange hurriedly left the area, he had sold his ranch for about one-tenth its value. Some heard that the Lagranges were moving to Mexico, but no one had seen or heard from them since their departure.

Wilson then decided to do some investigating around the old Legrange ranch for himself. He patiently and methodically searched the area for three weeks and found some buried ashes under a few inches of dirt near the house and around several peach trees. Among the ashes were charred and broken human bones, bits of clothing and buttons and teeth, "of which little was left but the discolored crowns." Wilson also uncovered shoe fasteners, a pocketknife with the handle burned off, a pair of eyeglasses and a suspender buckle. Most all of it was identified as the property of Steinbrook.

A second coroner's jury was summoned and ruled that "the evidence was sufficient to establish that a human body had been hacked to pieces at the Lagrange place; part of it buried, and part burned and scattered in various hiding places," the paper revealed.

However, the prime suspect, Lagrange, would not be located for another fifteen months. He had not moved to Mexico but instead was living under assumed names in Arizona. He and his wife wouldn't stay long in any one place, quickly leaving whenever they felt insecure. They were finally tracked down in the Pinal County town of Ray.

Police initially had no clue where to look for the suspects, but the case caught a break when Prescott resident Arthur E. Henry overheard in a conversation that Lagrange was residing in Ray under the name Anderson. He turned this information over to authorities.

C.E. Gilmer, sheriff of Gila County, who was on a leave of absence at the time, traveled to Ray to take a crack at the cold case and the $1,000 reward. Working off Henry's lead, Gilmer tracked down Lagrange, who was then living under the name Franklin.

Both Legrange and his wife were arrested for murder and sent back to Prescott. After Mrs. Lagrange was interviewed, her charges were dropped.

From the start of his trial, Lagrange's defense argued that it couldn't be proven that the remains were Steinbrook's. Witnesses testified that Steinbrook had a deformed foot due to a broken arch, but that foot was never found intact. At one time, his left arm had been broken, but that arm was also gone. He also had suffered a fracture of three ribs, yet those were the only three missing. Tellingly, the only parts of the corpse that were missing were the exact ones that could have identified Steinbrook!

Several witnesses for the prosecution stated that they owed Steinbrook money and that he never contacted them to collect it. Several more testified that they had appointments with him, but after the date of his disappearance, he never showed.

The defense "objected to any testimony directly connecting the charred and broken remains with Steinbrook," according to the paper, but Steinbrook's sister "was allowed to point out what she asserted to be peculiarities on her brothers head and similar peculiarities of the pieces of skull bones."

The second day of the trial proved dramatic. Lagrange took the stand in his own defense, "while an undertaker opened a basket four feet long and spread out on the table pieces of charred flesh from the torso of the man found in the bottom of the prospect shaft," the paper reported. The defense's reasoning for this ghastly spectacle was an attempt to prove that the remains were utterly unidentifiable.

Lagrange testified that Steinbrook had lived with him for nine months in 1920 and that they had parted on very friendly terms. Since then, Lagrange insisted that Steinbrook was still alive, returning occasionally to make whiskey. He quickly added that it was Steinbrook who made the liquor.

However, in light of the many witnesses testifying to his disappearance and the suspicious circumstantial evidence surrounding the missing body parts, Frank Lagrange was found guilty and sentenced to life imprisonment.

Lagrange appealed his case to the Arizona Supreme Court, citing the fact that the body could not be identified as Steinbrook's. However, the court decided that "there was a large volume of circumstantial evidence regarding the identification" of the body and ruled against Lagrange and upheld his life sentence.

Now, out of both options and hope, Lagrange began secretly making plans to escape prison. A scant two months later, he was afforded his chance. On March 28, 1924, while a heavy rain was falling on the prison at Florence, Lagrange "escaped without being observed by other prisoners or by the guards," the paper recounted. He was part of a crew that was painting in the prison yard. When the skies broke loose with a torrential downpour, Lagrange "concealed himself until [the] others had disappeared and then scaled the wall [before] heading to the hills." George Ruffner, Yavapai County sheriff, publicly opined that Lagrange may have had help from the guards, but he seemed alone among authorities. The guard who was found derelict resigned his position.

Mingus Mountain Inn

RING COPPER BELL FOR SERVICE

Please Help Yourself To The Salad Bar . . .
Take All You Want!

Connoisseur's Selection of Fine Wines

From the Char Broiler

Mountaineer T-Bone	6.95
New York Sirloin	5.95
Lobster Tail & Special Mingus Steak	7.50
Lobster Tail, Lemon Nut Butter Sauce	7.00
Filet Mignon, Bacon-Wrapped, Mushroom Sauce	5.50
Top Sirloin	4.95
Ground Sirloin, Mushroom Sauce	3.95
Hickory Cured Smoked Pork Chops	3.95
One-Half Broiled Chicken	3.25
Barbecue Beef Plate	3.50

✄ HOUSE SPECIALTY ✄

Baby Beef Liver, Rasher of Bacon	3.95
Sauted Sweetbreads with Mushroom Sauce	3.25
Veal Scallopini, Milano Style	3.75
Chicken Livers – Sauted, Fine Herbs	3.75
Filet of Sole, Butter Nut Saucier	3.95

The Above Entree Served With Your Salad Bar,
Pinto Beans, Home Baked Bread, Butter And All The Mountaineer Coffee
You Can Drink.

Bread to Take Home — 35c a Loaf

Open Daily 5:00 p.m. to 10:30 p.m. — Sundays & All Legal Holidays, Noon Until 10:30 p.m.

Rare picture of the menu at the old Mingus Mountain Inn, a restaurant and service station that used to be located at the summit of Mingus Mountain. *Drew Desmond collection.*

As soon as Lagrange was noticed to be missing, prison guards, a posse and a bloodhound were sent to search for him, but a week later, he was still on the loose. They had trailed him for fourteen miles southeast of Florence but lost his tracks. Eventually, the search was called off.

The "Christmas Butcher" who committed one of the most horrific murders in Yavapai County history was never recaptured.

15
TAKEN FOR A RIDE

By Drew Desmond

What do you say we go up and 'sap' this guy and take his car?" one man said to another. "I don't know why we can't get away with it. Nobody knows him up here. He just lives in that car."

Originally, they hired the driver to help them run some bootleg whiskey into Prescott for the upcoming World's Oldest Rodeo, Frontier Days, 1922. They "kept talking and talking," eventually planning to waylay the driver and steal his car.

It was about 1:00 p.m. when the illicit errand was completed and the two men, along with the driver, headed toward Groom Creek. On the way, they turned onto the Midnight Test Mine Road and parked two miles short of the mine itself.

Using some contrived excuse, one of the men convinced the driver to walk up the road with him, and they talked for a moment. When the driver turned and started walking back toward his car, the companion struck him over the head with a blackjack. He fell to the ground and murmured something, which only brought two or three more vicious blows to his skull. The assaulter then told his accomplice, "Now we got to drag him down this gully." To be sure that the job was finished, a knife was employed to stab the unconscious driver in the chest.

"Is he dead?" the accomplice asked.

"Yes," was the reply.

They rifled through his pockets and found only one dollar in change, a safety deposit box key and an accompanying bank account book. They also took the man's watch, his shoes, a five-dollar suit that had been purchased in Phoenix and a few other items police would uncover later.

The two then dragged the body to a cliff and threw it into the canyon below. "Well there is just one thing to do," the accomplice said, "and that is to get away." He would later confess to police that when they arrived back in Prescott, he was "nervous, half-drunk and in the damnedest fix in the world."

Twenty-five hours later, G.H. Herbert, who was camping in the vicinity of the Midnight Test Mine, decided to go for a hike, when he found the body near the side of the canyon wall. The man was unconscious and in dire shape. His eyes were swelled shut, "his head cut and bruised and battered almost beyond recognition," the *Journal-Miner* reported. Herbert notified the sheriff's office as quickly as he could.

When deputies arrived, the injured driver "roused up slightly and fought them in his delirium, until they handcuffed him and tied him down," the newspaper reported. The man was rushed to the hospital, and an investigation immediately ensued. Several small packets of a powdery substance, thought to be narcotics, were found around the unknown man. Looking up, the officers quickly noticed a quarter-mile trail of broken plants and dirt slides, showing the path the body had taken down the canyonside. The officers then proceeded up to where the man's fall had begun.

There, they found tire tracks, but no automobile. It was thought that the man's assailants drove him to the Midnight Test Mine Road, attacked him there, rifled his pockets and then threw him down the canyon, leaving a ghastly trail of blood.

The unfortunate victim was taken to County Hospital, where "Superintendent Fred Campbell said the man's condition was improving slightly and while he was still unconscious and unable to talk, it was believed he would recover, foiling the attempt of the would-be murderers who assailed him," the paper suggested.

Although mystery still surrounded his identity, the extent of the man's injuries was now apparent. In addition to the bruising and cuts from the quarter-mile fall, it appeared he had been beaten around the head and face and stabbed twice, just missing the heart, with one thrust piercing a lung. "Only the rugged constitution of the man saved his life," Campbell said. The man was described as "about 35 years old, weight about 185 or 200 pounds and more than 6 feet tall. His size alone prevented the knife from reaching his heart," Campbell believed.

The discovery of the powder packets led investigators to speculate that the man was a drug user or seller. "Whether the motive of the attack was murder, revenge, or robbery is to be determined by the investigators," the paper wrote, "unless the man revives sufficiently to tell the story himself."

It was the work of an astute *Journal-Miner* reporter that solved the mystery of the man's identity. He requested to see the drug evidence and found an overlooked prescription from the dispensary at Fort Whipple Hospital bearing the name Iver Enge. The reporter then approached the personnel officer at the fort, Michael Mahoney. Mahoney knew Enge and accompanied the reporter to the hospital. When Mahoney saw the patient, he thought it was Enge—he looked the same size, but his face was so badly mutilated that Mahoney couldn't be completely sure.

Finally, after two days, the man recovered just enough to barely whisper his name through his swollen lips. "Iver…Iver…," he said feebly.

"Enge?" he was asked.

"Enge…Enge…," was the breathy reply.

According to the doctor, Enge's pierced lung allowed air into his blood vessels, constricting his vocal cords. "Enge has a strong constitution and is making a mighty effort to live," he declared. "Nine men out of ten would not have lived more than 24 hours after the attack."

To make matters worse, Enge was also suffering from tuberculosis. The drug packets found around the crime scene had been prescribed for this malady.

Enge had been an orchard worker and was living in his car in Phoenix. He had made money driving people about for the previous two months. Before this, he had worked at Fort Whipple until his tuberculosis forced him to resign and seek rest. "Enge was a good work man," the paper related, "and was told that if he cared to return, Fort Whipple would give him a job if there was one vacant."

After several more days, the doctor was able to open one of Enge's eyes, since Enge was unable to accomplish that himself. He was then able to recognize Personnel Officer Mahoney and a former coworker at the fort. He also "regained enough control of his throat muscles" to swallow a little water.

"Two battles must be won by him before he can return from the shadow of the tomb," the paper observed. "First, he must overcome the demoralizing effects of shock and the loss of blood, and second, his body must throw off the air bubbles that the puncture in his left lung has permitted to filter into his blood vessels."

A week passed as Enge slipped in and out of consciousness. He recovered enough to finally open his eyes, recognize friends and begin writing feebly in response to questions. The first word he wrote was *milk*. It was provided immediately. However, he was unable to remember any details of his trauma and simply wrote his own name several times. When asked about what had happened to him, Enge did offer one clue: "Reif Hotel." Police investigated and found that Enge was supposed to meet a man there named William Acker.

Enge was then transferred to Prescott's Mercy Hospital, as Mahoney guaranteed his expenses. The citizens of Prescott were shocked by the crime and donated liberally for the poor man. They waited with anticipation for each day's newspaper to learn the latest concerning his condition.

While Enge's physical healing was sluggish, the regaining of his mental capacities was nearly stagnant. Two weeks after the attack, the newspaper reported: "Whether Enge himself will be able to reveal to the officers the names and description of his assailants and the story of his attempted murder, remain doubtful. He was reported at Mercy Hospital last night to be slightly worse."

Meanwhile, Enge's car was found wrecked in Maricopa, Arizona, and law enforcement connected it to William Acker (no relation to J.S. Acker, the Prescott businessman who donated parkland to the city). Although still unable to speak, Enge's writing improved. "His thoughts, however, [were] not directed toward his attackers, but...restricted to anxiety about his possessions," the paper noted. "When asked about Bill Acker and the mysterious drive out to the Midnight Test Road, he would reply in labored writing: 'Where is my car? Where are my clothes? Where is my bankroll? Where is my suitcase?' All efforts to elicit some response to the questions 'Who is Bill Acker?' and 'Why were you stabbed?'" proved fruitless.

The police tracked the movements of Enge's car and found witnesses who saw Acker driving it in Phoenix along with another unknown man.

Late in June, "a reward of $500 was offered...by Yavapai County for information leading to the arrest and conviction of William Acker, wanted in connection with the brutal assault upon Iver Enge," the paper declared.

Acker was eventually trailed from Phoenix to Los Angeles and arrested while in a restaurant on July 2. Police had shadowed him for three days, hoping he'd meet with his accomplice, but that did not occur. Acker, who occasionally went by the aliases "Doyle" and "Ehrhart," was rushed back to Phoenix to be held while awaiting his trial. Two deputies from Phoenix were joined by two Los Angeles detectives to make the arrest.

Once in custody, Acker confessed immediately. "He was quoted as saying he and his companion obtained the services of Enge to drive them in his car and that they beat him on the head until he became unconscious," the paper described. "Then his companion bared the victim's breast," and with a knife took aim at Enge's heart, "and twice drove the knife into him." They then tossed the unconscious man into the canyon below. The two men planned to take the car to California together, but after crashing it in Maricopa, they decided to go their separate ways. Acker went to California, while the second man said he was going to Colorado.

Acker denied taking part in the assault but admitted to the robbery. He was charged with highway robbery and grand larceny and was detained. At first, Acker claimed that he did not know his accomplice's name and later gave a false name in an effort to protect him. Further pressing from the police caused him to reveal it: Thomas W. Burge.

Acker was soon taken to Enge's hospital bed for a dramatic identification. When Acker entered the room, "Enge gave a faint smile of recognition and held out his hand," the paper reported. "Acker...trembled, drew white, and almost collapsed, but recovered and accepted the proffered hand," the paper said.

When Acker finally disclosed his accomplice's true name, police redoubled their efforts. Initially, law enforcement searched for him in California, but the trail was cold. Eventually, he was captured in Yuma after a twenty-five-day search that covered the states of Louisiana, Texas, New Mexico and Arizona.

When Burge was arrested, "a number of Enge's personal effects were found among Burge's belongings," including Enge's bank book. Immediately, Burge was subjected to a difficult "third-degree" interview by sheriff deputies. Despite being "confronted by [additional] evidence found at the scene of the crime, Burge did not bat an eye," the paper asserted, "claiming that they had the wrong man in custody. His arrest was due to mistaken identity, he told them."

The interrogators "admitted they were baffled by the man's composure." Burge even denied that he had ever known Enge, but records at Fort Whipple revealed that both were employed not only at the same time but also in the same building—one as a waiter and the other as kitchen help at the mess hall.

At the time of Burge's arrest, Acker was still awaiting trial. Law enforcement was wary about jailing them in the same place. "Once they get their heads together, they will catch up a story which will be difficult for the state to breakdown," an undersheriff explained. So, before bringing the two suspects together, Prescott police tried their luck at a harsh interrogation of Burge for the record, but were unsuccessful.

When the two suspects first saw each other in the sheriff's office, "neither showed signs of recognizing the other," the paper reported, "but as Burge was led from the room back to his cell…Acker turned to the officers present and said: 'Well, you needn't look any further; that's the man.'"

Both were denied bail.

Several weeks after the attack, it was decided to perform surgery on Enge to relieve pressure on his brain in hopes that his mental state would improve. However, the surgery failed, and he died five days later, having survived his terrible ordeal for a month.

After Enge's death, the medical examiner determined that the knife found on Acker at the time of his arrest "exactly fitted into the wounds of the dead man's left breast and shoulder," the paper reported. After this, Acker was taken from his cell "to a lonely shack where Enge's body had been laid out on a rough table. Acker was forced into the room with the corpse, and a light thrown upon the body."

"Why, why, that's Enge!" Acker said. This was the way Acker first learned of Enge's death and he immediately knew that his situation had become grave. The paper reported that Acker was "considerably shaken by the ordeal," and police began to give him "the third degree." Still, Acker did not deviate from the story he originally gave Phoenix police and reiterated that Burge was responsible for the assault and murder.

The charges now grew from grand theft auto and deadly assault to first-degree murder. Following a well-attended service at Ruffner's Funeral Chapel, Enge was interred in Mountain View Cemetery with former coworkers acting as pallbearers.

While investigating his estate, it soon became apparent that Enge had lived out of his car by his own choice. His assets, comprising mostly bank accounts, proved that the "poor man" was far more misfortunate than he was destitute. His estate was worth a surprising $10,000, which was three years' pay for the average man at the time.

At first, it was difficult to find an heir. "The Phoenix man, it appears, was a bachelor and the only known living relative is a sister, whose last address was Seattle," the paper related. "Seattle officers, however, have been unable to locate her." The next day, J.D. Porter, a friend of Enge's, appeared at the newspaper office with a trunk containing some of Enge's personal effects.

"Porter believes there is a sister living in Sweden and other near relatives," the paper declared, "and he intends to see that they have their rights. Enge once did Porter and his family a good turn of rather large importance at the time…and as a result, the entire Porter family cherished high regard for Enge and now they hold his memory as something worthy of their best efforts." The trunk was turned over to the administrator of the estate, who was able to locate an heir from information inside it.

As Acker's trial began, it was difficult to fill the jurors' box. "That the state will demand the death penalty for the alleged slayers of Iver Enge was indicated today when the jury panel was exhausted because of the number excused by the prosecution when they expressed objections to the death penalty and to circumstantial evidence," the paper stated. Acker "sat through the morning session and half of the afternoon session, apparently…unmoved, seldom glancing toward the jury box, but watching the prosecuting officials closely." The judge was required to call one hundred more prospective jurors to fill the box.

Even during the trial, Acker and his defense never swayed from his original confession, stating that he was a witness to the murder but that Burge did the killing.

However, most damaging to Acker's case was prosecution witness R.C. Ragsdale of Phoenix, who testified that Acker confessed to him that "not only was he present when Enge was attacked and fatally injured…but he himself administered the blows that caused Enge's death."

"We left Enge for dead, and started to drive away," Acker told Ragsdale. "I turned around and saw him trying to get up." Acker then related that it was he himself who finished the job, admitting that he got out of the car, hit the victim over the head with a blackjack and "stabbed Enge twice over the heart and once in the forehead."

When prosecuting attorney John L. Sullivan made his final argument for the death penalty, "Acker sat with a half smile playing over his lips. When the jury walked out of the box to begin their deliberations, he laughed," the paper reported. When a verdict of guilty, carrying the death penalty, was returned, "he received the announcement of the jury foreman apparently unmoved."

He was later sentenced to hang on December 1.

Attention then turned to the trial of Thomas Burge. He was about twenty-eight years old and stood five feet, eleven inches tall. He had sandy hair and a light complexion, with a small, dark mustache. His parents lived in Kinger, and his sister published a newspaper in De Ridder, Louisiana. He sent what money he could to his former wife, who was living in Colton, California, with his two boys, ages eleven and three.

Before his case came to trial, Burge attempted suicide in his jail cell. "Burge's suicide attempt was frustrated by Mrs. Ruth Merwin, county jail matron, who happened to pass Burge's cell on the top floor of the courthouse just as he was in the act of clawing at his throat with a broken [milk bottle]," the paper related. He lost a great deal of blood but fully recovered. "From now on, Burge will have a cellmate," Sheriff Dylan declared. "He will not be left alone for a moment."

The prosecution's case consisted of a parade of witnesses who testified to Enge's ownership of several items found in Burge's possession. Witnesses also testified that the alleged murder weapon, the blackjack, was sold to Burge "a few days before the attack."

The defense opened its case with Burge testifying in his own behalf. The courtroom was packed, but one seat was reserved for a special observer: his alleged and convicted accomplice, William Acker. "The impenetrable silence that Burge maintained during the days since his arrest was [finally] broken," the paper observed. Over the course of three hours, Burge told his story in a quiet voice. He admitted that he had met Acker and traveled with him the day after the alleged crime but completely denied that he had met Enge or had any knowledge of the assault.

He described his whereabouts on the day of the murder in minute detail. He insisted that he had never been on the Midnight Test Mine Road and that Acker picked him up in Enge's car after the assault, offering him a ride to Texas. Only when the vehicle broke down in Maricopa did Acker reveal that it was stolen, Burge insisted. It was then that the two men split, with Acker stowing away on the first westbound freight and Burge taking the next.

During cross-examination, Burge was queried about his attempted suicide. He explained that the cause was "depression due to the ill health of his father and his loneliness, and not his impending trial," the paper disclosed.

The paper described the defense's argument as: "No sensible person would leave so broad a trail." More profoundly, the defense produced two witnesses to corroborate Burge's testimony as to his whereabouts at the time of the murder.

Perhaps with some desperation, the prosecution desired to call Acker to testify against Burge. Against the advice of his own attorneys, Acker took the stand and repeated the story he had delivered many times before. However, the prosecution focused solely on the travel itinerary of the two and did not query Acker about the actual murder at all.

The jury was given the case at 8:30 p.m. the day before Thanksgiving. The following morning found Burge in his cell apprehensively awaiting his fate. At noon, the jury asked for clarification on some of its instructions and then enjoyed a turkey dinner prepared by a local restaurant.

Engine 3 passes through the Granite Dells. *Courtesy WikiMedia Commons.*

Shortly after 4:15 p.m., the jury announced that it had reached a verdict. In attendance was Burge's sister from Louisiana and his two sons. The boys were kept just outside the courtroom as the verdict was being read: "We the jury, duly impaneled in the above entitled cause, upon our oaths, do find the defendant not guilty."

"Oh thank God!" Burge's sister exclaimed as she rushed to his arms. His sons rushed in and "embraced him with rough joy," the paper described.

The children declared that "they were going to 'take their daddy back to Louisiana and there would be no more trouble.'"

It seemed Burge and his supporters were willing to use any available means to keep him off the gallows. In an interesting sidelight to the trial, Burge's uncle D.O. Dunn was arrested for trying to bribe one of the prosecution's witnesses. It was James Todd, who would testify that he sold to Burge the blackjack used to beat Enge. Dunn had bought a railroad ticket to Gallup, New Mexico, and offered it to Todd along with a sum of money. However, police had been tipped off; at that very moment, sheriff deputies swooped in and arrested Dunn.

Despite the evidence against him, Dunn's defense was compelling enough to win him an acquittal after the jury deliberated for thirteen hours.

It was also found that one juror in Burge's case, named Millard, lied about his qualifications in hopes of being seated. Arrested in early December 1922, he had been unable to produce the $2,000 bail and stayed in jail until the following year, when a new county attorney declined to prosecute the case and released him.

Acker was sentenced to hang on December 1, but an appeal was granted, and he was kept in the Yavapai County jail. When his appeal was lost on May 24, 1924, he was sent to death row in Florence and sentenced to hang on August 8.

In light of Burge's exoneration, the public immediately lost its appetite for Acker to pay with his life, and a campaign for commutation began. In mid-July, Acker's parents came to Prescott to plead for their son's life. They won the support of prosecuting attorney Sullivan as well as Judge Sweeney, who had sentenced Acker to death. Petitions were circulated around town asking the Arizona Parole and Pardons Board to commute his sentence. Unfortunately, Acker's aged parents couldn't afford to stay long and were not able to address the board.

However, when the time came, Judge Sweeney and John Sullivan were joined by former sheriff Joseph P. Dillon, several jailers and nine members of the jury, which had returned the verdict of guilty against Acker. The board noted that "various clergymen and numerous businessmen…[also] joined in this prayer."

After hearing the appeal, the parole board was deadlocked but "working toward a decision." By then, the gallows for Acker had already been built, but the parole board desired to hear from Acker himself, so Governor George Hunt delayed the execution another month. The paper described the move as "one of the most important developments in this spectacular fight to save Acker from the gallows."

Mining stock certificate for the Lucky Strike Copper Company. *Courtesy www.visitwhc.org.*

After interviewing Acker, the board decided to sign a recommendation to Governor Hunt suggesting leniency. The board was convinced that Acker was guilty of first-degree murder but was moved by the citizens' outcry to save his life.

For Hunt, it was an easy decision. He had shown opposition to the death penalty by commuting several death sentences at the outset of his first term. Although a handful of those proved controversial, he had plenty of political cover to act in Acker's case.

After receiving the news "emotionally," Acker's first request was for Prison Superintendent R.B. Sims to send a telegram to his parents informing them that his life was saved. "Acker, overjoyed and expressing thankfulness, became so unsteady that he was unable to eat his evening meal," the paper reported. "Acker also asked Sims to convey his heartfelt thanks to the Governor, to members of the Board of Pardons and Paroles, and to the friends who fought for weeks to save him from the extreme penalty."

Now sentenced to life in prison, Acker settled into a job as a main hall chef, due to his past experience at Fort Whipple.

His crime was the first homicidal carjacking in Prescott's history.

16

FORMER BOXING MANAGER BEATS HIS WEALTHY FRAIL FRIEND TO DEATH

By Bradley G. Courtney

I t was one of the few times a local murder commanded the top headline in the *Prescott Evening Courier*. In fact, the bloody deed and the subsequent trial were headlined repeatedly in May and July 1938. It was even picked up by the Associated Press and reported in the *New York Times*.

In the very early morning hours of May 11, 1938, Ernesto Lira beat to death his friend Marcus Jay Lawrence inside Lira's house at 104 Grove Street. The incident stemmed from a love triangle among the two men and Odessa Webb. Lira was arrested later that morning and charged with first-degree murder the next day. The trial, which took place in July of that year, captivated not only Prescott but also the entire state and attracted standing-room-only crowds that extended into the Yavapai County Courthouse hallways.

Marcus Lawrence, described in newspapers as a "Verde man," hailed from a wealthy and prominent Washington, D.C. family. His mother, Carrie J. Lawrence, was a social leader in the capital city and "an intimate of many prominent people." In 1931, Lawrence bought the V-Bar-V Ranch, a dude ranch on Beaver Creek near Verde Valley, because he wanted to be a cowboy.

Lawrence went in with his best friend, Bruce Brockett, who became manager of the ranch. Formerly the Minotto Ranch, it was renamed and improved by the two of them, and they "erected a magnificent home nearby." Lawrence's wealth stemmed from a trust fund of $700,000 (more than $12,000,000 in today's money). He was receiving $5,000 a month (roughly $90,000 today) from it and had money to burn.

Over time after his death, Marcus Lawrence was portrayed as a ladies' man. During Lira's trial, the defense accused him of being a "homebreaker." A more recent article about Lawrence called him an "infamous Verde Valley playboy." However, his friends described him as a "shy, retiring, courteous and kindly gentleman, somewhat broken and discouraged by matrimonial misfortunes" and was generally considered a "good fellow."

Lawrence's purported reticence came from a lack of self-confidence and a speech impediment that compelled him to avoid people. He also shied away from any ambitions relating to financial matters. Physically, he was a slight, almost frail man.

At the time of his death, Lawrence was still technically married to Jane Stout Lawrence of Illinois. The couple married in Washington, D.C., in March 1936. However, Jane had recently filed for divorce in the Yavapai County Superior Court, alleging that he was habitually intemperate. This may have been true. Today, there are those still living in Prescott who remember Lawrence as an inveterate gambler and drunk.

Yet Bruce Brockett, as close to Lawrence as anyone, claimed that he had never seen his friend drink anything stronger than beer while married. That changed, he admitted, after Lawrence's wife sued for divorce. Lawrence repeatedly attempted to reconcile with her but was rebuffed to the point that, in order to try to forget his sadness, he left the ranch and sought out the lights and nightlife of Whiskey Row.

Lawrence met Ernesto Lira, a naturalized Italian, in 1934 at a rodeo in Long Valley, Arizona, some eighty miles east of Prescott. Perhaps a year before that, Lira met Odessa Webb. In 1933, they began posing as Mr. and Mrs. Lira, although they were never actually married. A friendship grew among Lawrence, Ernesto and Odessa, and the trio soon became "an almost constant companionship." There were numerous card games at the Palace Saloon or Bungalow Café, dinner parties and trips to the Grand Canyon and Albuquerque. Many times, they just met for drinks and conversation.

While Lawrence was facing marital difficulties, he, at Lira's invitation— and, more often than not—stayed at the couple's house, so much so that Brockett feared he would not return to the ranch. The middle bedroom in Lira's house, in fact, was often referred to as Lawrence's room. Odessa often stayed in the front bedroom, which shared a wall and a door with the middle bedroom. Lira apparently at times did not share his own room, the back bedroom, with Odessa, although she kept some clothes there.

During the course of the trial, Lira tried to gain sympathy from jurors and appear the victim of the "homewrecker" Lawrence, stating that he was "a friend I took into my home and treated like a gentleman." Lira also claimed that Lawrence thanked him and Odessa for saving his life, because, when going through his marital struggles, there were times Lawrence wanted to die. Lira said that Lawrence told him that their friendship had rescued him: "I give you and Odessa all the credit for that and for treating me so nice."

Physically and in terms of personality, the forty-year-old Ernesto Lira was the opposite of Lawrence. He was a larger, more powerful man with an outgoing, charismatic way about him. He also had a deep knowledge of the "sweet science," having served as manager for the light-heavyweight champion of the world, Hall of Fame boxer John Henry Lewis. In 1931, Lewis, then sixteen years old, inadvertently killed Sam Terrain with a punch to the heart during a boxing match in Prescott that Lira had promoted.

Born in a little town in Italy on November 13, 1897, Lira came to the United States when he was sixteen with his father and a cousin. Initially, he lived in Trinidad, Colorado, working in the coal mines near there and in New Mexico. Lira was also a talented trumpeter and played in a mine company's band. He moved to Prescott in 1924 and lived in several places, at first in the Palace Hotel. He eventually became a pinball and amusement-game operator and a hotel manager. For a period, he traveled to Paris and Italy, playing his trumpet in theaters and concert halls while keeping a home in Prescott.

Later, unproven rumors circulated that Lira was a Yavapai County "underworld boss." During his trial, a key witness, Undersheriff Bob Born, testified that although he had been friends and partied with Lira in the past, he eventually told him: "I have always had trouble with you. You are always on the opposite side from the law." No details were given as to what Born meant by this.

One surviving old-timer believes that Lawrence owed Lira a hefty sum of money from gambling. The prosecution tried to prove that this was why Lira beat Lawrence, not because of his love for Odessa. According to a mutual friend, George "Big George" Voun, who had been friends with Lira for fifteen years and had recently come to know Lawrence and Odessa, it was indeed usually Lawrence who lost during the card games they played. In fact, Lawrence had recently lost $1,500 (valued today at more than $25,000) in one sitting. Lira, Voun said, usually broke even, and he himself usually came out ahead. However, he also maintained that Lawrence often partnered with Lira during the high-stakes games.

Denying the claim that Lawrence was invited to play in these card games because he was wealthy and could be taken advantage of, Big George testified that Lawrence was never asked to play. He joined in willingly. And when drinking, Lawrence became a free spender.

Yet there is evidence that Lawrence had become involved with Prescott's shadier elements. During the July trial, Bruce Brockett dropped a bombshell. In early 1938, he had warned Lawrence that there were racketeers in town "who were trying to take him." Brockett had visited Lawrence at the Lira home, hoping to coax him back to the safer environment of the ranch.

Another attempt was made when Lawrence brought Lira and Odessa to his ranch. Brockett was there and able to get Lawrence alone to again urge him to return home. Lira himself said he would help Brockett in his efforts.

Odessa Webb, just twenty-seven years old at the time of Lawrence's death, became such an infamous, yet intriguing, Prescott figure that when headlined and spoken of in Prescott newspapers, only her first name was given. That was all readers needed to identify her. During Lira's trial, she was referred to as "the woman in the case." Whenever she testified, those in the courtroom—80 percent of whom were women on most days, it was reported—craned their necks to get a look at the beautiful woman and hung on to every word she spoke.

Odessa had been posing as Lira's wife for five years. For three of those five years, she was still legally married to Everett Webb.

Odessa freely admitted that she and Lawrence had become intimate, that their relationship had gone past friendship. They had various meetings in Prescott and once spent the night together in Cottonwood. Odessa, according to her testimony, called Brockett while at a bar there and lied to him that she was on her way to Winslow, although confessing that she had met Lawrence in Cottonwood. It was a plant to cover herself, because she was planning to spend the night with him, she said.

Odessa's testimony was contradicted by Brockett. He asserted that during that conversation, she told him, "I've got him. What should I do with him? Shall I hang onto him?" She denied ever saying this. Although it would have no bearing on Lira's trial, Brockett's claim was backed by the bartender of the Cottonwood bar, Bob Francis, and a patron, W.M. Horsford.

Lira first became suspicious on Friday, May 6, that his pseudo-wife and Lawrence were having an affair. It appears the two lovers were careless at times, perhaps impaired by alcohol. Lawrence had called Lira to ask him to pick up some aspirin for Odessa that day, as she was not feeling well. When Lira came home, the two were in the living room on a davenport. Odessa was sitting up, but Lawrence was partially inclined. What made Lira scratch his head, however, was that Lawrence's pants were unbuttoned.

On Saturday, May 7, there was another davenport incident, but no details were given.

Lira decided to spy on the two to find out if more was going on. On Sunday, May 8, he told them that he was heading to Whiskey Row for some drinking and gambling. Instead, he parked his car in the alley behind Grove Street, crept onto his back porch to the kitchen window and tried to see and hear what was actually going on when he was out of the house and assumed to be downtown. He had a partial view of the living room and a clear view of the davenport.

During his trial in July, Lira testified, "I saw Odessa come out of the bedroom and sit on the davenport where Marcus was lying and then I saw Marcus put his hand around Odessa's hip." This caused him to move close to the living room window, where he heard Marcus ask Odessa, "You're mine, aren't you?" Odessa's reply was, "Well, not yet. Maybe in a while." He then moved back to the porch window, through which he saw Odessa clad in pajamas. It appeared that Lawrence was fully dressed.

Lira returned to his car and drove to Whiskey Row. Returning home later, he walked through the front door and into the house to find two towels near a bedroom door, as if Odessa and Lawrence had taken a shower together. He spotted Lawrence lying on the davenport and Odessa hurrying to the bedroom. He asked no questions, and no words were exchanged.

During the night of Monday, May 9, Lira resumed his spying. This time, he went into Whiskey Row with Big George Voun, who had made dinner at the Lira house that evening for everyone. At some point, Lira left Voun and once again parked his car in the alley behind Grove Street.

This time, Lira attempted to go straight into the house but found the porch door locked. Moving to the window of Lawrence's bedroom, he could hear them talking but was unable to understand what was being said. Lira then went to the front bedroom door and began pounding. There was no answer, so he tried the front porch door. Still no answer.

Lira went back and forth to bang on each door. Odessa finally answered after five minutes. Lira could tell that she had hurriedly dressed. Lawrence was sitting on the davenport donned only in shorts but was clamoring for a bathrobe. Lira attested, "I asked him what he wanted a bathrobe for when he had been alone in the house with my wife with only his shorts on."

But that was it for the night. No further conversation ensued, and the three retired for the night. Later, Odessa asserted that Lira essentially condoned the intimate feelings she and Lawrence had for each other. She spoke of the instances when Lira found them in compromising situations and declared that "Lira made no serious trouble about them." Lira did not see it that way and felt that he was being misled. Indeed, evidence leads to the certainty that Lawrence and Odessa tried to hide their relationship from Lira.

Lira's suspicions were reaching a peak. During the morning of Tuesday, May 10, Odessa's twenty-seventh birthday, he set a trap. Lira placed a scrap of paper in the latch of the door between Lawrence's and Odessa's bedrooms and later returned to find it lying on the floor.

For the first time he confronted Odessa, accusing her of going into Lawrence's bedroom where he had been in bed. She told him that no such thing happened. Lira did not challenge Lawrence, but he was becoming obsessed with catching them in the act. On the same day, Lira bought a camera and flashbulb and hid them under his bed while Lawrence was napping in the middle room.

A joint birthday party took place at the Lira home that night for Odessa and her friend Mrs. M.A. Russell. Odessa and Big George prepared the dinner. When it came time to eat and party, Lawrence was still asleep. Lira teased him, telling him that he was going to throw him into the shower and douse him with cold water if he did not get up. Lawrence got out of bed and brought out a birthday cake with candles for Odessa. Lira helped him light the candles.

The party ended around 11:00 p.m. Odessa and Russell cleared the table and changed clothes, and they both left around midnight for some drinks on Whiskey Row. Lawrence was to meet them later. At one point, when everyone else was on the Row, a taxi was sent to Lawrence, but he refused it and climbed into bed.

Voun said that Lawrence had been drinking but did not appear to be intoxicated. In fact, both Odessa and Voun claimed that Lawrence drank less that night than the others. Lira and Big George left together for some drinks as well, but after a short time, Lira, having made other plans, left.

He rushed to Tivoli's Club, a dark and dingy place on the west side of North Cortez Street, where Lira told the bartender to tell anyone who called—and he apparently expected that call to come—that he was there but too deeply involved in a card game to be disturbed. Little did that bartender know that he would inadvertently become an accomplice to murder.

Then Lira returned home. He took off his shoes and sneaked into his house so quietly that Lawrence did not notice. He waited in the back bedroom for Odessa's eventual return.

Odessa and Russell had started at the Bungalow Café, then went to the Palace for drinks and were seen by Big George sitting at the famous bar. Voun was looking for Lira but, failing to find him there, stopped into Tivoli's. Odessa and Russell accompanied him there. Lira was not there, either. Odessa and Russell went back to their respective homes while Voun stayed downtown.

As soon as Odessa entered the house, she removed her shoes and promptly called the Tivoli Club to see if her pretend husband was now there, which she hoped would be the case. The bartender, as instructed by Lira, told Odessa that he was but was caught up in a card game and unable to come to the phone.

Unbeknownst to Odessa and Lawrence, when Lira heard Odessa in the house, he grabbed the camera and hid in his closet. If what he suspected was true, he wanted a photograph to prove it. Deep down, he knew he was being duped. With proof, he could confront them. On the face of it, that is all Lira had initially planned.

Feeling assured that she and Lawrence were alone in the house, Odessa went into Lira's room and grabbed her pajamas while her "husband" was in the closet. Lira heard her come in; at one point, they were two feet away from each other. Lira next listened to Lawrence call out to Odessa to come to his room. She answered that she would be there in a minute and went into the front bedroom and changed. Lawrence was nude and waiting in his bed as Odessa entered. He got out of bed, and they greeted each other with an embrace and a kiss.

After hearing Odessa's reply to Lawrence, Lira tiptoed out of the closet and his bedroom. Through the partially opened door of Lawrence's bedroom, he could see the two lovers standing up and kissing. He then went through the living room and into the front bedroom, intending to hear their conversation through the wall and connecting door, but their words were indistinct to him.

Eventually, the two climbed into bed together, with Lawrence sitting up while Odessa laid across the bed. They talked for nearly a half hour—Odessa admitted that they were also kissing—but the fear of Lira returning home and getting caught intensified for both of them. Again, Odessa got up and phoned the Tivoli Club and was given the same answer as before. Lira was still playing cards, the bartender said. Just around the corner from her, Lira was hiding in the front bedroom.

Believing they would be alone for a while longer, Odessa climbed into bed with the nude Lawrence. However, knowing Lira could come home any minute as had happened the night before, she told Lawrence that she was going to fetch him some pajamas—which for some reason were in the front bedroom—in order to look less suspicious. She came through the room's door, and there waiting was an angry Lira, holding his camera.

"Now I have you together. Let's hear you explain this!" shouted Lira. Lawrence and Odessa begged Lira to believe there "was nothing wrong."

"What do you mean? Do you say I am a liar?" Lira bellowed.

Then all hell broke loose.

The camera became not a chronicler of their affair but a weapon. Lira later told Big George that he "lost his head." On the witness stand, a very nervous Lira made an incredulous claim about that moment when all of his plans suddenly and dramatically changed: "Then something like a streak of lightning went through me and I hit her and knocked her down." Perhaps this was an illusion to him, because both stated that the flashbulb in the camera went off in her face at the same time she was hit. The prosecution derided Lira's "streak of lightning" claim, calling it pure absurdity.

Lawrence stepped in. Now Lira was attacking both of them, Odessa with his fist and Lawrence with his camera. Although claiming that he did not intend to kill Lawrence, he admitted that he hit him with the camera over and over "as hard as he could." If not intentional murder, the former boxing manager was sending his friend a very serious message that would not be forgotten. He kept shouting at Lawrence, "I don't see how you could do me this way?!"

At one point, Lira said that he "missed" Odessa, so he turned back toward her. She was the center of his wrath once again, and he resumed beating her, knocking her down time after time. Odessa tried to run out of the room to the outdoors, but Lira kicked her back to the floor. Lawrence tried to divert Lira away from Odessa by heading toward a stack of guns in the corner. He grabbed a shotgun, which caught Lira's attention. The two men began struggling for the weapon.

Odessa was now teetering between consciousness and unconsciousness, but she remembered the scuffle for a gun. Lira vaguely remembered what happened at this point but said he knew he eventually knocked Lawrence down. He told Undersheriff Bob Born, "I remember struggling over the shot gun but don't remember hitting him with it."

Yet bloodstains were later found on the barrel and butt of the gun. Odessa claimed that, at one point, she had tried to wrestle the gun away from Lira but was knocked down. It was never clear whose blood was on the gun. During the preliminary hearing in May, she had said that she had been knocked out by a hard object. Curiously, she denied that statement during Lira's trial in July.

Lira's next-door neighbor John Beach was awakened around 2:00 a.m. by shouting and slapping sounds. From his kitchen window, he had a view into the front bedroom. He could see Lira in front of the bed. Lawrence and Odessa were on the floor. Odessa attempted to get on to the bed, and under it, several times, but Lira knocked her back to the floor, once grabbing her by the feet and throwing her to the ground. Beach also testified that Lira repeatedly yelled, "I caught you in bed together!"

Lira landed one more blow, sending Lawrence toward the ground. He hit his head on the baseboard and fell unconscious. Lira stated that this was when "I came to myself."

Suddenly, the fighting was over.

Beach next testified that Lira, after seeing the damage he had wrought, ran frantically back and forth from the bathroom to the front bedroom with a washcloth. Odessa had a vague memory of Lira bringing her hot towels.

In a bizarre twist, Lawrence shook hands with Lira at some point as if the matter had been settled between them. According to Lira, Lawrence even apologized for betraying him, saying he "would do anything in the world to make things right."

Lira got Lawrence into the bathtub to clean him up. He applied iodine to Lawrence's wounds, hoping to stop the bleeding. It did not. Lira testified that he told Lawrence that a doctor should be called, but Lawrence asked him not to do that. He was embarrassed and wanted to keep the matter private, as if that was now possible.

Having stayed out into the wee hours of the morning, Voun had returned to the Bungalow Café and while there was summoned to the phone. It was Lira asking Big George to hurry to his house. The hysterical Lira provided no details.

Arriving on the scene around 4:00 a.m., Voun found a house in shambles. Papers were strewn across the living room floor, as were bottles, glasses and cigarette butts. There were bloodstains all over the walls and floor and on pillows, clothes and linens. Lira's camera was in pieces. The shotgun that had been fought over was dismantled—perhaps inadvertently during the struggle for it—but bloodstains were evident on the butt and barrel.

On the phonograph player, two songs were cued: "The Touch of Your Lips" and, ironically, "Keep Away from My Door." The birthday present to Odessa from Lawrence was found among the shambles in the front room: "a beautiful cigarette case with a birthday card from Lawrence therein." There was also an empty pistol holder with the pistol located in another room. The other guns were seen, but none of them had been discharged recently.

Voun saw Lawrence covered in blood. "I entered the living room," he testified, "and went on into the front bedroom a few steps. Lira was standing against the wall to my left as I entered and Odessa was on the bed. Lawrence was sitting against the east wall and on the floor." He asked Lira what had happened. Lira gasped, "I lost my head," and then told him why. Voun expressed disbelief and then attempted to wash the blood from Lawrence. He asked Lira if he had summoned a doctor, and he said that he had.

Dr. Ernest Born, brother of Undersheriff Bob Born, arrived and attempted to gain control of Lawrence's bleeding. He realized he needed more medical supplies and made a trip back to his office to gather them. After his second visit, however, Born inexplicably went home.

Did Lawrence repeatedly resist being taken to the hospital? During Lira's trial, the defense severely criticized Born for leaving the scene, to the extent of blaming his negligence for Lawrence's death. He would be accused of "leisurely" traveling back and forth to Lira's home to treat Lawrence, not recognizing the obvious urgency at the time and ignoring the possibility that there was "bleeding in the brain cavity itself." There was also the issue of not sending Odessa to the hospital.

After Dr. Born departed the second time, Odessa was still lying in bed, barely conscious and terribly battered. She later said she could barely remember the doctor treating her or even that Voun was there. Lawrence, feeling sleepy now, stood up and, without saying more, stumbled back into bed and lay down.

At some point, Voun left the house. There was clearly a stage when it was hoped that everything would just smooth out, that the whole matter would be kept private, paid no heed, that Lawrence and Odessa would heal and that life would go on as usual after a spell. Big George remembered that Lawrence asked him, "Please don't say anything to anyone about this."

Voun returned around 8:00 a.m. to find Lawrence still in bed. Lira was lying on the floor in a semihysterical state, asking himself, "What have I done?" Things were looking bleak.

Shortly after, there was a third visit by Dr. Born. Lawrence was now quickly slipping away. He fell unconscious.

Dr. Born finally decided that Lawrence should be taken immediately to Mercy Hospital, just up the road on Grove Street (today the location of the Prescott College campus). Born asserted that he had done "everything possible to bring Lawrence out of his unconsciousness, but to no avail."

After Lawrence had been moved to the hospital, Sheriff George Ruffner arrived. Asking the panicky Lira what had happened, the former boxing coach's first response was, "Oh, my God!" Eventually, Justice of the Peace Gordon Clark came to the house. So did attorney Charles Ewing, who would become Lira's prosecutor. Ruffner overheard Lira saying: "I just as well tell you. I'm only going to tell the truth!"

Ruffner said that he saw Odessa in bed covered up. Lira was having trouble walking and lay down on the davenport, and later next to Odessa. After Ruffner placed his hand on Lira's shoulder, Lira asked the sheriff, "He isn't dead yet, is he?"

Ruffner answered, "Yes, he just died."

Lawrence was dead on arrival and may have died in the Lira home. The time of death was given as 8:45 a.m. Three and a half hours had passed since Dr. Born first began treating Lawrence.

Lira voluntarily gave himself up.

Lawrence's beaten body was sent to Ruffner's Funeral Home and displayed to coroners. "The frail body showed deep cuts and contusions about the head, bruised lips and some bruises on the arms," reported the *Courier*. Dr. Born designated "the cause of death as cerebral concussion and hemorrhage, due to blows from outside sources." Altogether, seven wounds were counted.

That afternoon, Odessa was taken by friends and secluded with them. She was unable to speak about what had happened. Severe bruising was evident all over her body, and both eyes were swollen and blackened.

On Thursday, May 12, the silent, unshaven, visibly worried but well-dressed killer allowed a photographer to take his picture in jail. Lira was promptly charged with first-degree murder. On that same day, Odessa was taken to a cell and held as a material witness. Mrs. T.L. Burch, Odessa's aged and frail mother, sat with her daughter behind bars the entire night.

On Saturday, May 14, the $5,000 bond was paid on Odessa's behalf. She walked out on her own power and was taken to her mother's home. When able to talk, Odessa said she did not know how she survived the beating.

Lawrence's mother, who had been aboard the SS *Reliance*, was contacted in the canal zone of Panama. She would not be coming to Prescott. Instead, she directed that her son's body be immediately shipped to Cleveland, Ohio, his birth city. John Martin, attaché to the family, would escort the body.

Lawrence's estranged wife, Jane, and her mother arrived from Phoenix and stayed at the Hassayampa Hotel to keep an eye on developments.

On July 16, after a ten-day trial, Lira stood with downcast eyes as he listened to the verdict. He was guilty of second-degree murder. The jurors took three and a half hours to reach that conclusion, believing there was no

Unknown prisoner at the old Yavapai County jail. *Courtesy Sharlot Hall Museum.*

premeditation on Lira's part. Sentencing was to take place on July 30. Most locals expected fifteen to twenty years, the maximum for second-degree murder at that time.

On the day of sentencing, Lira stated, "I told the truth at my trial. It was an accident. I didn't intend to kill Marcus. Marcus was my friend. I've regretted it ever since. I'll regret it all my life." Then he hung his head and waited. The throng inside the courtroom gasped when they heard the sentence of thirty to forty years. He was sent to the prison in Florence, Arizona.

While serving his sentence, a photograph of Lira next to a boxer he was managing in prison was published in Tucson's *Arizona Daily Star* on February 14, 1939. He looked dapper and even happy with a cigar hanging from his mouth.

Apparently, the length of the sentence was all for show. Although an Arizona statute existed that did not allow a convicted prisoner to apply for parole until the minimum of a sentence was served, Lira was released after five years. He was not allowed to enter Arizona again, even though he attempted to get permission to return in 1947. His early release would be used later that year as an example during an Arizona senate debate over a bill that would enable early releases for prisoners through work performed during imprisonment.

On the day of Lira's sentencing, Bruce Brockett filed charges against Odessa for "open and notorious cohabitation" with Lira—in other words, adultery. These were the days when it was thought that common morality could be enforced and crimeless immorality legally punished. Odessa spent one night in jail before a $1,000 bond was posted for her. Eventually, charges were dropped.

Odessa remarried in less than a year's time to a former Prescott businessman, J.R. Rawson, and the couple moved to Flagstaff. Odessa appeared in a newspaper again in March 1939. Her husband had been arrested in Winslow for writing a bad check for thirty-five dollars to Flagstaff's Monte Vista Hotel. Prescottonians found it irresistible to keep their tongues out of their cheeks. "She sure knows how to pick 'em," wrote one pundit.

Soon after Lawrence's death, his widow, Jane Lawrence, filed a petition in hopes of becoming the administrator of her deceased husband's very substantial estate. She was denied. Because she had filed for divorce, it "rendered her antagonistic towards the estate and not a fit person to act as administrator thereof." He left behind $700,000 (worth over $12,000,000 today). To his mother went $200,000. His brother, Paul, received $100,000. Jane Lawrence was given the minimum permitted by law at that time to a widow. Where the remainder of his money went was not reported.

On June 5, 1939, just short of thirteen months after Marcus Lawrence's death, the *Courier* reported: "To perpetuate the memory of her son in the part of the world he best loved, Mrs. Carrie J. Lawrence, of Washington, D.C., will build and liberally endow a free clinic for indigents and medical research in the town of Cottonwood." On October 29, 1939, the Marcus J. Lawrence Memorial Clinic was dedicated and formally opened. Less than two years later, the clinic was expanded. On April 29, 1941, it became the Marcus J. Lawrence Memorial Hospital, remaining so for almost fifty-eight years.

As the years passed, Lawrence's name grew in notoriety—in much the same way that Ernesto Lira's defense portrayed him during the trials of 1938—as a drunk, out-of-control gambler and, most of all, a homewrecker. Some believe that he was viewed as the type of person whose name should not be attached to a hospital. On March 10, 1999, the name was changed to the Verde Valley Medical Center.

Ernesto Lira died on April 30, 1966, at the age of sixty-nine in San Joaquin, California.

ABOUT THE AUTHORS

Drew Desmond is a Prescott historian and author of the *#PrescottAZHistory* blog, which features over two hundred articles and has welcomed over a half-million readers. He is also secretary of the board of the Prescott Western Heritage Foundation and spends several hours welcoming visitors to its Western Heritage Center on historic Whiskey Row. Drew was first charmed by Prescott while on a business trip in 1998 and moved there in 2002. He has spoken about Prescott history to various groups and schools and spends his free time sightseeing and in the great outdoors.

Bradley G. Courtney, author of *Prescott's Original Whiskey Row* and *The Whiskey Row Fire of 1900*, is an independent historian who lived and taught in Phoenix, Arizona, for nineteen years and on the Navajo Indian Reservation in northern Arizona for twelve years. For six of those years, he was also a riverboat pilot and guide who gave tours down the incomparable canyons of the Colorado River. Brad has also recorded three albums of original music and has appeared on CNN, the Travel Channel and numerous other television outlets across the country. He holds a master's degree in history from California State University.